Energize Your Business

"Ray is a talented writer who truly believes in his writing and practices that every day through his work. He is a genuine person who wants to make this world a better place."

~Jerry Simmons, Managing Partner,
INDI Group

"It is with great enthusiasm that I highly recommend Ray to any business interested in facilitation, strategic planning, or leadership coaching. Ray served as the facilitator for the Gilbert Chamber of Commerce Annual Board Retreat and did a tremendous job of keeping our group focused and action-oriented. We had a limited amount of time to prioritize an action plan and build consensus. I'm pleased to say we were able to accomplish this with Ray's expertise and skills to draw on the strengths of the group."

~Kathy Tilque, President/CEO,
Gilbert Chamber of Commerce

"I have known Ray for over 20 years, and I suppose all that time, he really has served as my 'life coach.' However, more recently, we have formalized our relationship to consult on a regular basis regarding all my business endeavors. Let me assure you: Ray understands the laws of success and will help keep you on the path. I read all the great books and understood everything in them about success, but when it comes to the details of YOUR OWN business life, you will not believe how cunning your mind can be, justifying all sorts of thoughts and feelings that feed your ego but take you off the path of success. That's where Ray comes in. You'll hear truth from him, and you will move forward toward realizing your greatest dreams."

~Chief Master Bill Babin,
ATA 8th Degree Black Belt and Business Owner

"If you are looking for a dynamic, inspiring guest speaker, workshop leader, or Board facilitator, Ray Madaghiele is your man!"

~Joel Baehr, Past President,
Unity Worldwide Ministries

"We all truly appreciate the way you made a usually tedious and difficult process seem so easy. Your facilitation was well prepared, your delivery polished, and the end result speaks directly to what we all had in mind."

~Duane Black, former C.O.O., SunCor Development
Co-author, *The Hands Off Manager*

"The Salt River Pima Maricopa Indian Community worked with Ray on 10 different occasions, at various levels of the organization in strategic planning and teambuilding. Ray's facilitation style and approach works very well for us. I recommend Ray for any organization that embarks on the Strategic Planning journey."

~Bryan D. Meyers, Community Manager
Salt River Pima-Maricopa Indian Community

"Beginning with a Statement of Values, a Mission Statement, and a Purpose Statement, you have guided us through the wholesale revamping of our Strategic Business Plan and helped us identify our strengths and weaknesses. This guidance has strengthened the foundation of our organization..."

~Lynn Kusy, former Executive Director,
Phoenix-Mesa Gateway Airport

"It was Ray who taught me that through teamwork we can accomplish incredible things…Ray is a person of integrity. He is someone I trust, respect and admire. He is creative and works hard both professionally and in his service to the town."

~Hon. Cynthia Dunham, former Mayor, Town of Gilbert, AZ
Executive Director and Founder, The Leadership Centre

"Ray is a thoughtful professional who helps his clients realize their potential to be better organizations, leaders, and managers. He utilizes the right blend of technical insight, organizational management, and personal development tools to foster positive and strategic growth. A man of integrity and action, Ray is a dependable professional who delivers quality work products."

~Casey Denny, Vice President,
Asset Management, Columbus Regional Airport Authority
Past President, Southwest Chapter of AAAE

"Ray Madaghiele (Ray of Hope) is an experienced speaker and proven business leader with a strong history of delivering dynamic, entertaining and interactive, keynote speeches and/or training sessions to a wide range of organizations. His many years of transformational motivational speaking energize and provide practical and innovative solutions. Ray's training programs cover a wide range of subjects including Communication, Leadership, Organization, Team Work, and Commitment. My personal experience with Ray is that his effective delivery is exceptionally well-polished and charismatic, which engages the audience while providing a safe and relaxed ambiance."

~Deb Schwalm,
Self-Employed Artist

"Ray is an engaging person who is down to earth and has a tremendous appeal to his audience…

Your remarks were meaningful, entertaining, and inspirational; and your dynamic manner of presentation resulted in getting your points across to the audience. I was particularly impressed with how well you 'worked the room' in your presentation. Your ability to make your audience have fun, while probing some deep subjects are an outstanding combination.

Through your message and approach with audience participation, you captivated their attention throughout our session… which wowed the group of approximately 50 upper-level airport human resources and financial professionals from all over North America… who in turn gave you the highest ratings possible for your presentation."

~Nancy Zimini, Sr. VP Administration & Operations,
Airports Council International-North America

"You're amazing! I really appreciate your help and commitment on this project. You got us to produce lots of ideas, and that will help us greatly going forward."

~Greg Tilque, President, Gilbert Sister Cities
Senior Economic Specialist, Greater Phoenix Chamber of Commerce

"I met Ray when he facilitated our Board's Annual Planning Retreat. He was excellent at this—very focused on taking us from where we were to considering new ideas together and coming to some helpful conclusions. Since that time, we have had other times we have partnered in a project or event. He is organized, pays attention to detail, is always so pleasant to be around, and the end results are really great. I have the highest regard for Ray and his work ethics and would tell anyone who has the pleasure of working with Ray that they are in for a wonderful experience!"

~Anne Taylor, Business Manager,
Arizona Interfaith Movement

"This book will provide you with a jumping off point and a kick-in-the-pants to get energized and take action to make your own organization better. Ray is a great facilitator, trainer, and coach who has helped our leadership team move forward together with a common understanding, direction, and focus of what we want to achieve as an organization. Ray has provided us with many valuable tools to make us a better organization and better people both inside and outside our agency."

~Leo Huppert, Contract Manager
Arizona Cooperative Therapies

Energize
Your Business

Engage Your Employees
with an
Inspiring Strategic Planning Process

Secrets from a Master Facilitator

Ray Madaghiele

Inspiring Hope ~ Awakening Greatness

ENERGIZE YOUR BUSINESS

Engage Your Employees with an Inspiring Strategic Planning Process

Copyright © Print Book 2015

by Ray Madaghiele

ISBN 10: 0-9787097-3-X (Print Book)

ISBN 13: 978-0-9787097-3-0 (Print Book)

Published by

Transformational Learning Center (TLC)

Sioux Falls, SD 57104

Previous books by Ray Madaghiele

10th Anniversary Edition titled *Ray of Hope: Inspiring Peace—Insights on Chaos and Consciousness while Bicycling Across America*, printed 2012

First edition printing under the title *Ray of Hope for Peace: Insights on Chaos and Consciousness while Cycling Across America*, September 2004

This book is dedicated to all the passionate business owners who have the courage to take a leap of faith to act on their dreams.

This book is also dedicated to my wife, Lyn, and my sons, Dominic and Joe, who have endured and supported me on my business journey since 1995 as I have followed my passion.

Table of Contents

Acknowledgments

Thank you, Lyn, my soul mate and compassionate, candid sounding board, and first-level editor.

Thank you, Jerry Simmons, for your publishing wisdom and coaching direction with this lofty book project.

Thank you, Paul McNeese, for your editing mastery and discovering the right and perfect words to express what is in my heart and mind.

Thank you, Signe Nichols, for taking my raw manuscript and bringing it alive as an attractive, inviting print and eBook.

Thank you, Brian Hankes, for creating a book cover that captures perfectly the complete essence of the message of this book.

Thank you, Steve Harrison, Joe McAllister, and Martha Bullen at Bradley Communications for offering the Bestseller Blueprint Program, and for your coaching insights early on in this creation.

Thank you, SCORE and ASBA mentors and teachers, for providing me with the tools and encouragement 20 years ago to make my dream of owning a business a reality.

Thank you, Starbucks Team at Signal Butte in Mesa, Arizona, for "inspiring and nurturing my spirit" with the perfect environment to write this book.

Thank you to those business owners who honored and entrusted me to share your inspiring stories with the world: Thom Coker, Johnny "Cupcakes" Earle, Leo Huppert, Bryan Meyers, Mike Smith, Victor and Christina Thompson, and Margie Traylor.

Thank you to those of you who shared your candid and helpful viewpoints to design a valuable book to help businesses thrive and dreams come alive: Casey Denny, Cynthia Dunham, Larry Grossman, Joe Hitzel, Leo Huppert, Amber Neubauer, Carla Royter, Sarah Pingatore, Brian Sexton, Greg and Kathy Tilque, and Bob Wilson.

Thank you, my readers, for choosing to purchase this book to make your business dreams and aspirations a reality.

Preface

"If you fail to plan, you are planning to fail!"

~Benjamin Franklin
Inventor, Business Owner, and Statesman

Ray facilitating a community group in Prescott, Arizona

Enjoy exploring Ray's website!
http://www.energizeyourbusiness.biz/

Since you are perusing *Energize Your Business*, you are probably thinking about doing a strategic plan for your organization. My guess is that you compared the volume and weight of other books on the subject and decided to browse through this one to see if a book with less than half the pages could deliver the same results with less work. That is my goal—to simplify the process so that a business leader like you can quickly *get clear, get organized, get going, and get results*™.

When I created my first organizational and human excellence company in 1994, I, too, looked for a good book on strategic planning but soon discovered most to be heady and complicated. I could care less about learning a new and complex language, studying academic research, or applying lengthy processes.

I simply wanted to *get clear, get organized, get going, and get results*™ as quickly as possible.

"Get clear, get organized, get going, and get results!"™

If that's what you're looking for, this is the book for you.

Unfortunately, the experience many people have with strategic planning resembles a definition I heard several years ago when I attended a seminar on strategic planning. The speaker characterized the strategic planning process as "a painful, boring, dreaded-but-necessary evil," while I sat there thinking, "No! It doesn't have to be that way!" Then he talked about the process being "the sole responsibility of the top leaders in the organization." Again, I thought, "No, no, no!"

If your experience parallels mine, I invite you to keep reading to discover a much more inspiring and fun approach. Yes, even fun!

A strategic plan done *right* will inspire its participants and leave a lasting, positive impression. It may even be life-changing.

For example, while I was writing this book I coincidentally bumped into a former client in a restaurant. I spotted Mike Smith, owner of Jokake Companies, and decided to say hello. He was meeting with a partner for a new business venture.

Without skipping a beat, Mike shared with me how important a strategic planning retreat a colleague and I had presented to his leadership team in 1999 had been for him and his organization. In fact, he opened the notebook on the table in front of him to show me that he still carries with him the purpose, mission, and values we guided his team to create sixteen years ago. What came next blew me away. Completely from memory, and without even glancing down at his notebook, he repeated their heartfelt purpose statement: "*to touch those we serve, and transform dreams into reality.*" Wow! I'm sure my mouth was hanging open. Then, what Mike said next really hit home: "*This has essentially become my purpose in life, too. During our retreat, you brought in the spiritual side of the planning process, which really catapulted it to a higher level than we had ever had before, and we still operate at that same level.*"

What if your strategic planning process could be this memorable and durable?

The truth is, planning is vital for the success of your business—no matter how many employees you have. And it has also been my experience that *your employees care more about the success of your company—and are smarter—than you think*. Every one of your employees has something to contribute to the process, irrespective of what his or her role in the organization may be. Why? Because everyone wants to be a valuable part of something meaningful.

---

*"All people desire to be a valuable part
of something meaningful."*

I have come to believe that a strategic planning process done well . . .

- is an engaging, inspiring and fun opportunity to create collaboration and cooperation among all employees
- creates alignment from the top of the organization to the frontline—getting everyone moving in the same direction toward the same vision and common goals
- does something unexplainable—it invokes a natural law of attraction, attracting the right and perfect

- employees and customers, people who resonate with your organization's culture and aspirations
- energizes and lifts your organization and everyone in it to the next level of success and fulfillment!

"A strategic planning process done well…
is an engaging, inspiring and fun opportunity to create
collaboration and cooperation among all employees."

A strategic plan is similar to a trail map for trekking in the wilderness. When taking a hike into unknown territory, it is helpful to locate your starting point, identify your desired destination, and decide on the route that will best enable you to enjoy a fun adventure while still making the trip safely and successfully. Along the path you may discover and investigate new and exciting excursions that you wouldn't have experienced if you hadn't begun your journey. Even if you decide to deviate from the planned route, your map (strategic plan) will still help you to use good judgment as you blaze a new path.

Of course, when venturing into new territory there will always be uncertainty and discomfort at first; but, over time, the new path will become more recognizable, increasingly comfortable, and easier to travel. It will truly become a new, exciting adventure, perhaps even beyond your wildest dreams.

During my twenty-five years of facilitating strategic planning processes for a wide variety of organizations and communities, I have heard many myths about strategic planning. You may even believe some of them yourself.

Myth #1: Small business owners don't need a strategic plan unless they intend to get money from investors or banks.

Myth #2: Strategic planning is boring drudgery to be tolerated, much like swallowing awful-tasting medicine that's good for you in the long run.

Myth #3: The strategic planning process is a hard, complex, heady process that only someone with an MBA could possibly appreciate and understand.

Myth #4: Strategic planning is an esoteric process, reserved for leaders in Fortune 500 companies and created on corporate "mountain-tops". Then management delivers the completed tablets to its loyal subjects in the form of new laws to follow.

Myth #5: Employees have more important things to do than to waste time planning. Besides, frontline employees don't care about planning and have very little to contribute to the process anyway.

Myth #6: Strategic plans are just nice pronouncements that collect dust on a bookshelf, to be opened again only at next year's company retreat.

From my experience, these myths are far from the truth. As you continue reading, you will discover a new set of truths that will better serve you and your organization.

This book is designed to be a trail map for you, as a leader or potential leader of a small- to large-sized business, to guide you toward creating your own strategic plan, which will ultimately become both the map and the compass for your organization. You may have limited experience with strategic planning or have little time to spend on a lengthy process. Therefore, this book is streamlined to enable you to get clear, get organized, get going, and get results as quickly as possible—so you can get on with operating your day-to-day business.

Energize is structured in four phases:

- In the 1st Phase, you will learn *what* will cause your team to **get clear** about the direction to take the organization and *why* to do it;
- In the 2nd Phase, you will learn *what* will motivate your team to **get organized** and be on the same page, moving in the same direction, and *why* to do it;
- In the 3rd Phase, you will learn *what* will cause your team to **get going** efficiently and effectively with implementing your action plans and *why* it's important to keep the plan alive;

- In the 4th Phase, you will learn how to ensure that your teams **get results** that exceed your desires and expectations; and

- The last section provides a **Step-by-Step Facilitator's Guide** that reveals my time-tested secrets for how to set the right energy for the strategic planning process and how to facilitate each element so as to produce amazing results.

Throughout *Energize*, I will share my secrets and proven, practical tools and tips accumulated over my 25 years of experience facilitating groups. You will read stories and examples of successful companies who have implemented the very principles and processes discussed in the book.

Long before you've finished reading this book you will discover that strategic planning is not rocket science. The planning process, as we at TLC envision it, has been streamlined and written in a conversational style that makes it easy to understand and implement for any sized business—without needing to learn another language.

My hope is that you will see strategic planning as one of the best ways to truly engage your employees in the success of your organization and just how easy, fun and inspiring the process can be for everyone involved.

If this is what you're looking for, I think you're going to find *Energize Your Business* a valuable tool for taking your organization to its next level of success.

Enjoy the journey!

Ray Madaghiele
Chief Inspiration Officer and Master Facilitator
Business Energizers, a division of
Transformational Learning Center
Inspiring Hope ~ Awakening Greatness

Introduction

"Less than one-third (31.5%) of U.S. workers were engaged in their jobs in 2014."

~2014 Gallup Poll
of 80,837 U.S. working adults over 18 years old

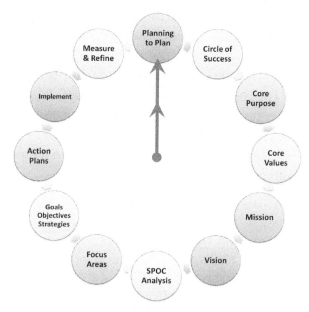

Figure 1:
The 12-step Strategic Planning Process
to Engage Your Employees

Employee engagement has been an emotionally potent buzz phrase during the past decade—but what truly engages people? The secret is to involve your employees in something meaningful, inspiring and lasting, such as a strategic planning process.

Here's something significant that I learned from a Native American community about ten years ago. On a frigid December day in northern Minnesota, I was facilitating a strategic planning retreat for the Leech Lake Band of Ojibwe. More than 75 people from different departments within the tribal government were meeting in small groups in the ballroom of one of their casino enterprises. I was introducing elements of the strategic planning process, step-by-step, and the participants were storyboarding their input on flipcharts at their tables. Many of the participants had never been asked to participate in a strategic planning process like this before, so part of my time was spent teaching and coaching about the different elements.

Two hours into the morning of the first day, Vicki, a leader from their Education Department, came up to me on a break and shared a metaphor of the tree, relating it to the strategic planning process. It described perfectly the significance of each element of the process and how each is related energetically and how all are connected to the whole system.

That night I captured her thoughts in the graphic shown in Figure 2, "The Tree of Organizational Success." That tree became our guide for the next several days of our process. People got it! Since that day, I have continued to use it as a tool to guide groups in their strategic planning processes. Here's the essence of what she shared with me.

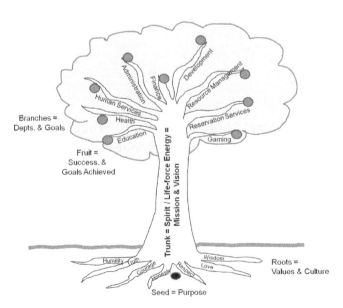

Figure 2: The Tree of Organizational Success

Seed = Purpose

Every tree begins with a seed. The tree exists within the seed. Each seed has a specific, unique purpose. A pine-cone seed can grow up to be only a pine tree. An acorn can grow up to be only an oak tree. An apple seed can grow up to be only an apple tree. Every organization has a unique core purpose for how to serve the world. This is "the big why?"— the reason the organization was started in the first place—beyond just making money.

Roots = Values

With the right amount of sun, water and minerals from the earth, the seed begins to sprout roots. Roots help to nourish the tree by drawing water and minerals up from the soil. They also help to stabilize the tree against external forces like wind and floods. Roots also stabilize the tree within the surrounding soil, which can become weak from erosion. Roots are invisible to the eye, but they serve the tree in several other important ways. The deeper and wider the root system, the more nourishment the tree will receive. Roots represent the core values and culture in an organization. They are what your organization stands for. They are your legacy. The more widespread and deeply imbedded your core values, the more likely it is that your organization will stand the test of time.

Trunk = Spirit / Life-force Energy = Mission and Vision

When the tree's roots spread out and deepen enough, the tree begins to sprout and break through the surface of the earth. It first becomes visible as a delicate sprout that eventually forms the trunk. As the tree grows tall for all to see, its life-force energy and spirit becomes evident.

The trunk of the tree is analogous to the mission and vision of an organization. Everyone can see and experience the magnitude of its energy and presence. The mission and vision are the life-force, or spirit, of the organization. Many will be prospered, served and inspired during the life of the organization.

Branches = Departments and Goals Set

Branches bud and spread out from the trunk in all directions. These branches will support the foliage and fruit that will come.

The greater the reach of the branches and canopy, the more fruit the tree is capable of producing. It soon begins serving animals and insects—providing shade, food and refuge.

The branches symbolize the various departments and the multiple goals of the organization. The loftier the goals set throughout your organization, the greater the potential for organizational and personal achievement. As personal growth trainer Les Brown says, "Shoot for the moon; and if you miss, you will still be among the stars."

*"Shoot for the moon; and if you miss,
you will still be among the stars."*

Fruit = Success and Goals Achieved

As fall approaches, the world begins to see apples form on an apple tree. You—and the world—can now see how plentiful the harvest will become, weather and critters permitting. The fruits of your labor are becoming visible.

The fruit harvest represents goals achieved, success manifested. A bountiful harvest serves your customers, employees and vendors.

I love the simplicity and organic perspective that I received from my student (and teacher), Vicki, that day.

As the result of my work with Native American communities throughout America, I have learned that very few things evolve in straight lines connecting A to B—most actually unfold in a more dynamic, complex circular fashion. Since I am an engineer by training, I have found that this is also true at a quantum energy level. Even chaos is a sign that transformation is occurring. As a matter of fact, chaos is the perfect time for transformation.

In my management experience, I have come to understand that the strategic planning process is no different. As I guide you through a linear, step-by-step strategic planning process, I will frequently remind you to build in circles of flexibility so that your own process can expand naturally, both to suit your organization's unique needs and to respond to the marketplace. As your organization moves through the planning process, you will most likely experience a degree of chaos just prior to breaking through to reaching consensus. Fear not. This is natural. This is a good indication that transformation is unfolding. The greater the chaos, the more significant will be the transformation.

"Build in circles of flexibility so that your own process can expand naturally to suit your organization's unique needs and to respond to the marketplace."

Creating Strategic Alignment

What I love about a well-done strategic planning process is that it accomplishes collaboration and cooperation throughout your organization. Having everyone participate in the process naturally creates enthusiastic buy-in and support all the way from the top tier of the organization to the frontline. (See the Strategic Alignment Model in Figure 3 below.)

Figure 3: The Strategic Alignment Model

Energize Your Business will first define the elements of the strategic planning process in an easy-to-understand, conversational way and then guide you, step-by-step, to take on the role of lead facilitator for your organization. And if you would rather hire a professional than to self-facilitate, I will provide you tips for choosing the right and perfect change agent for your organization.

You and your employees will understand the steps for getting clear, getting organized, getting going, and getting results quickly toward your organization's next level of success—getting the results that you seek.

The Strategic Alignment Model shows what's possible with respect to involving more and more people in the process as it unfolds. It is a natural, cascading effect—similar to water flowing down terraces in a mountain stream. In the beginning, the top leaders of the organization define and agree upon the core purpose of the enterprise. Then, middle-management becomes actively engaged with the top leaders in creating the relevant values, mission, vision, goals and strategies, with further input and constructive review from other frontline leaders. Next, the top leaders and middle-management engage frontline leaders in establishing the tactics and beginning the action plans. Then, the frontline leaders engage their staff such that every employee is empowered to give detailed input to complete the action plans. And finally, departments and their individual workers establish personal goals and tasks which can now be tailored to accomplish some element of the overall strategic plan as part of each participant's Individual Development Plan (IDP).

By the end of the process, your organization will be crackling with energy. Everyone will be involved. You and your employees will feel energized. By involving everyone in the process, you will naturally earn your employees' enthusiastic support and buy-in because they will realize that they are an integral part of creating your new direction. It will not be just *your* plan. It will be *everyone's* plan. Everyone will have a vested interest in the success of the organization. That's what true ownership is.

"By involving everyone in the process, you will naturally earn your employees' enthusiastic support and buy-in."

My hope is that this book will energize and inspire your hope and faith in what's possible for your organization and that it helps you to awaken the greatness in your teams to achieve it.

So, let's get clear, get organized, get going, and get results!

1st Phase: Get Clear

"Strong deeply rooted desire is the starting point of all achievement."

~Napoleon Hill
Author, *Law of Success* and *Think and Grow Rich*

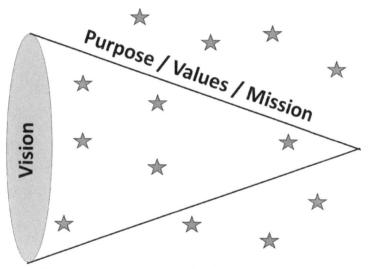

Figure 4: The Cone of Influence (Get Clear)

During the 1st Phase your employees will aspire to reach new heights with a clear picture of what you are striving to achieve as an organization.

During this first phase you will explore the purpose, values, mission, and vision that form the "Cone of Influence" of your organization. These elements define the depth and breadth of what is important to your organization. The more lofty your vision, the wider your Cone of Influence.

The stars represent potential opportunities to expend or invest resources. Any stars outside the Cone of Influence represent those you should not include in your planning. They are not in alignment with the direction and focus of your organization. Those stars within the Cone of Influence represent opportunities that you could develop or undertake, depending on available resources. These are opportunities in alignment with what is important to your organization.

You and your employees will answer questions like: Where are we now? Why are we here as an organization? What do we stand for? What is the business we're in or about? What does our company look like in its desired future state?

Chapter 1

See Where You Are

"A journey of a thousand miles must begin with a single step."

~Lao Tzu
Wise political ruler of the 5th Century B.C.
and Author, *Tao Te Ching*

Remember that a strategic plan is like a trail map and compass for hiking in the wilderness. But to begin any journey, you first need to know where you are—which is to say that before you begin any strategic planning process it is good to evaluate how you are presently maximizing the potential of your organization.

If you are anything like me, simple visual assessments let me know quickly how I am doing in leading my organization.

For example, next year you will most likely be taking a vacation. If you are traveling by car, one of the first things you will probably do is check the air pressure of your tires. The last thing you want to do is drive on a deflated tire, right? A tire doesn't have to be flat to cause problems. A tire low on air can heat up and eventually blow out or, at the very least, increase fuel consumption and costs. Yet that is exactly what many leaders are doing. Many leaders are trying to run their organizations with "flat spots" that decrease productivity, produce inefficiencies, and impede growth.

> *"Many leaders are trying to run their organization with*
> *"flat spots" that decrease productivity,*
> *produce inefficiencies, and impede growth."*

Here's a simple assessment tool for you and your employees to see the "flat spots" in your organization and where you are maximizing your potential. It is an organizational medicine wheel that I call the Circle of Success. (See Figure 5.)

I have been using this simple, yet revealing strategic planning tool for many years with the organizations I serve. It provides leaders with a quick visual assessment of many of the ingredients that breed success and profitability in organizations. It's also a great, engaging teambuilding exercise.

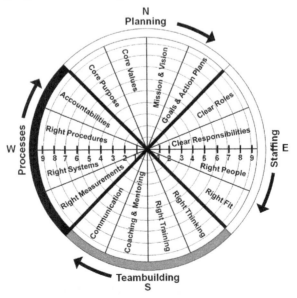

Figure 5: The Circle of Success

In a nutshell, when you can maximize each of these sectors, you will be maximizing your organization's potential.

In general:

- when each of the "Planning" sectors is well-defined and clear to all your employees, everyone will be on the same page and moving in the same direction;

- when "Staffing" your organization, you hire the right people, assign them to the right jobs, and know that they have a clear understanding about their roles and responsibilities;

- when "Teambuilding," your employees have been given the right training, coaching, and mentoring so that they will make the right decisions; and

- when you have established the right "Processes"—measurements, systems, procedures, accountabilities, etc.—you will have primed your organization and employees to succeed in serving your customers.

I invite you to give it a try. I think you will like its simplicity and the visual impact it will have on you and your leaders. It is a most effective way to see where you need to focus energy and resources (the flat spots).

So, how well does your organization's wheel roll?

See the **Step-by-Step Facilitator's Guide** in the last section of this book for more detail on how to use the Circle of Success Assessment tool.

Energizing Thoughts to Ponder
for Chapter 1

1. In which sectors of the Circle of Success does your organization excel?

2. In which sectors of the Circle of Success does your organization need the most improvement?

3. Answer #1 and #2 above for each separate department to get the full picture of specific areas to focus energy and resources.

Chapter 2

Remember Your "Big Why?"

"Cause and effect, means and ends, seed and fruit, cannot be severed; for the effect already blooms in the cause, the end pre-exists in the means, the fruit in the seed."

~Ralph Waldo Emerson
American essayist, lecturer, and poet
who led the Transcendentalist Movement

A wise grandfather, sitting in the shade of an apple tree on a sunny, fall day, was telling ancient stories to his seven-year-old granddaughter, Mary. He picked up a fallen apple and held it up for Mary to see.

"Where did this apple come from?"

"From the tree, Grandfather!"

"Yes, Mary, and before that, from a seed."

Then Grandfather drew his knife from its sheath on his hip, took the apple in his hand, cut it in half, and handed both sections to Mary.

"Tell me how many seeds are in this apple," he said.

After a minute or so of picking the seeds from the apple core, she replied, "Seven, Grandfather."

"Good, Mary."

He then took a single apple seed from the apple, placed it on a rock, and cut it in half.

"Open your palm, Mary."

He placed both halves of the seed in her palm.

"Now, tell me how many apples are in this seed?"

Mary looked perplexed as she stared at the seed. After several moments of silence she replied, "I don't know, Grandfather."

"That's true, Mary. No one knows. You can count the number of seeds in an apple, but you can't count the number of apples in a seed. Only the Creator knows how many apples a seed will produce during the tree's lifetime."

"You can count the number of seeds in an apple, but you can't count the number of apples in a seed."

The core purpose of your organization is like the seed of an apple. No one knows the potential yield of your organization and how much your employees can produce in the lifetime of your company.

Your organization has a unique core purpose for serving the world. This is your "Big why?"—why your organization was started in the first place—beyond just making money. What's yours? It is most likely the original heartfelt reason you decided (or are deciding) to take a leap of faith and start a business.

Knowing your core purpose keeps you centered on what's most important—during good times and challenging times.

"Knowing your core purpose keeps you centered on what's most important—during good times and challenging times."

Recently I attended a Small Business Development Center (SBDC) awards event held on the Arizona State Capitol lawn, where I met a charming couple who started a business together— Christina and Victor Thompson. They shared their unique story with me.

It was a night like any other in 2011; but by morning, Christina and Victor's life together would change forever.

Deep into her night's sleep, with her husband and three girls tucked snugly in their beds, Christina had a vivid dream. When she awoke she remembered every detail of her dream so clearly that she could almost see, touch, taste and smell it. Every one of her senses was alive. Joy and excitement filled her soul.

She waited patiently for her husband to awaken. He immediately noticed Christina's bubbling excitement. Here is what he shared with me about his recollection of their conversation.

> *Christina immediately shared her dream. It had so much detail about a concept she had for a business! She described a concept that I'd never heard of—all about an "eco-chic environment"—a place where people can go to relax and get manicures, pedicures and facials without being exposed to toxins; a place where people with allergies, chronic illnesses, pregnant moms, or just a health-conscious consumer could go to be pampered and not be exposed to hazardous chemicals. I had never heard of such a concept, especially in Tucson, Arizona. She even knew the name. Greentoes.*
>
> *I asked her, "Is anybody doing this?'"*
>
> *She replied, "I don't think so."*
>
> *I immediately told her, "That sounds like a strong concept and idea. You're going to have to do that!"*
>
> *That morning, Greentoes was born.*

That very day, Christina moved into action, beginning her research and development to see if anything like it had been created yet. She applied the organizational skills she had developed as a master, award-winning teacher (which had been her focus for 16 years). In the same way that she defined objectives and outcomes for her class curriculum, she defined clear, specific objectives for every facet of the business.

Fueled by passion and driven by a clear core purpose to create an *Eco-Chic Mani Pedi Studio and Day Spa*, Christina followed each of her days at her teaching job with evenings dedicated to breathing life into her business plan. Victor was amazed at what she was able to accomplish in just a few months.

Even more amazing was the response from the vice-president of their bank when Christina presented her business plan to get funding to start the business. The banker told her it was one of the best, clearest, and most thorough business plans he had ever seen. He was amazed that she didn't have prior business experience or training. He referred her to the Tucson, Arizona Chapter of the Small Business Development Center (SBDC) to give her direction and mentoring on the steps for starting her business.

From the moment of Christina's dream to the Grand Opening of Greentoes, it was a mere ten months.

Suddenly, however, the trajectory of Greentoes shifted. Victor shared what happened next.

> One part of Christina's dream was also that she needed to slow down—that something was going to change in her life. And also that I was to be involved.
>
> Three months after opening the business, she became very sick with the Multiple Sclerosis (MS) [that she had learned to live with since 2000]. One evening she was in pain and I was helping her take a bath. That's the night she sprang the news on me.
>
> She said, "Hey. We have to talk about a couple of things. I have to stop working."
>
> I said, "Okay!"
>
> "You don't understand," she repeated. "I have to stop working."
>
> I said, "Okay. When are you going to stop teaching?"
>
> "No. You're not getting it! I have to stop everything. I have to stop Greentoes. You need to take over Greentoes."
>
> When she told me, I was totally caught off guard. I was like, "What? Na ah. No way! I don't know anything about this business."
>
> My support up to that point had been working with

Gene [Christina's father] to put everything together inside the building. [At that time Victor worked with Gene in his remodeling business].

I told Christina, "I don't know anything about the business. I didn't do the business plan or the research all those months. I don't know anything about the product. You're kidding me, right? How are you expecting me to do this?"

As we were talking she looked me in the eyes and said knowingly, "You can do this!"

I looked down at the floor shaking my head no. At this same time I'm thinking, "Okay, I've worked with subcontractors in the contracting business; I've run jobs, but mostly I thought these two things: (1) She said, 'You can do this!' and (2) I just don't want Christina's dream to die."

I went up to her, waved my hands in her face to get her attention, looked her in the eyes and told her, "I'll take care of it!"

Remembering your core purpose provides the strength and focus you need to get through the tough times. It helps make the tough decisions easier. Knowing your core purpose helps you stay heart-centered on what is most important.

"Knowing your core purpose helps you stay heart-centered on what is most important."

When Victor looked into Christina's eyes on that fateful evening, he could feel his fear melt away. In his heart, in that moment, he understood that he needed to keep Christina's dream and the purpose of Greentoes alive.

He continued to work with the counselors at the SBDC to learn the next steps of their business.

Yes, Victor did learn how to run an *Eco-Chic Mani Pedi Studio and Day Spa*. Even today, Victor comes home excited to share the latest colors of nail polish with Christina. He shared,

"I had to learn a lot of new stuff about oils, salt scrubs, lotions

and even something called 'Cutie Cocktail' for making your nails stronger [laughter]."

Together, Victor and Christina have created a thriving, high-end experience with lofty employee and customer service standards, all centered around a strong core purpose.

Greentoes opened its doors in 2012 as scheduled, with a $40,000 personal investment; and the business earned $11,000 the first year. The spa has six employees and generated revenues exceeding six figures in 2013, doubling that in 2014. An expansion is planned for 2015.

Greentoes won a 2015 Success Award from the Arizona Small Business Development Center for its unique and excellent business practices and growth.

As Christina and Victor learned, amazing things unfold when you dare to dream and begin with a clear purpose in mind and heart.

"Amazing things unfold when you dare to dream and begin with a clear purpose in mind and heart."

Today, Christina gets to enjoy the harvest of the seed she planted many years ago—free spa treatments to support her own health and well-being.

Remember when you first got excited about the idea of starting your own business—when you got goose bumps just thinking about it? Where were you? What was *your* inspired idea that grew into *your* "big why?" for doing it—beyond just making money? The answer is something very simple and profound at the core of your mission as an organization.

This is the core purpose of your company. It should be at the heart of everything you do, all the decisions you make. It is why your organization exists. It either solves a problem or fulfills an aspiration or desire. It is the seed that, when properly nurtured, will begin to take root.

Once you and your employees understand your core purpose and have placed it at the heart of everything you do, everyone involved will make good, sound decisions. It will be a compass for all you choose to do.

Here are other examples of core purposes from successful companies that you might know:

- Disney – "To bring happiness to millions"
- Nordstrom – "Service to the customer above all else"
- Johnson and Johnson – "To alleviate pain and disease"
- 3M – "Innovation...thou shalt not kill a new product idea"
- Walmart – "We exist to provide value to our customers"
- GE – "Improving the quality of life through technology and innovation"
- My company, TLC – "We inspire hope and awaken greatness"

What's the Core Purpose of your organization?

To facilitate the discovery your organization's Core Purpose, refer to the **Step-by-Step Facilitator's Guide** in the last section of the book.

Energizing Thoughts to Ponder for Chapter 2

1. What do you think is your organization's Core Purpose? Why does your organization exist—beyond just making money? What solution to a problem or need is your organization fulfilling? Take some time to journal some possibilities.

2. What do you think is your organization's ultimate potential?

3. What do you think your employees believe the core purpose is?

4. What do your employees think is the ultimate potential for the organization?

Chapter 3

Infuse Your Culture

"The only truly reliable source of stability is a strong inner core [purpose and values] and the willingness to change and adapt everything except that core."

~Jim Collins & Jerry Porras
Authors, *Built to Last*

What does your organization stand for—your core values? Here are a few business owners who understand how vital a company's core values are to creating a company culture that results in happy, productive, successful employees, which, in turn, leads to happy customers and a healthy bottom-line.

Margie Traylor and Bret Giles created Sitewire in 1999 after becoming disenchanted with their jobs. They knew that they could create a better, more engaging organizational culture. In 2014, they employed 65 employees, billed $25 million, and over the years have won numerous awards and praises from prominent business journals. Margie is also giving back by serving as Treasurer for the National Board of the Service Corps of Retired Executives (SCORE), the organization that provided her with initial coaching for starting their business. See more about SCORE in the "Free Resources" section at the back of the book.

Margie shared Sitewire's story with me, beginning with why she decided to start a business.

I had become an armchair quarterback in corporate America. I was tired of watching others struggle as leaders. The company [that I was working for] lost its way with their core business. Instead of taking ideas from their employees, they started bringing in consultants. They weren't listening to us. I became very disillusioned with some of the decision-making. That company eventually went bankrupt. I thought I could do it better.

Then something happened that became my catalyst for making the decision to start a business.

My dad was trained as a portrait artist but never had a chance to do that because he was so busy earning money to feed six kids. He was 62 years old, two weeks from retirement. He walked out the door at 4 a.m. to paint more billboards, and he died. My dad never got a chance to pursue his dreams.

His death was the kick in the pants that I needed. When he died, I decided it was time for me to pursue my dreams. I was 34 when he died. I looked at him and realized that he never took the time to live his dream. He only chased after money—not that it was the most important thing in his life—but he had six kids and he had to. So, I sat back and realized that I don't want my life to go that way. I want to—while I'm young enough—go pursue my dreams. And my dream was literally to go out there and prove I could be a better leader than some of the ones I had seen.

I found a business partner that I could work with incredibly well (Brett Giles). We were pioneers in e-commerce and saw a market opportunity for us to pursue. Both my business partner and I were unhappy at [our jobs]. We decided to give it a go to see if we could do it better.

In our early years, we got awarded a lot for the way we ran our business. We were Fortune Small Business Best Bosses award recipients. We were SBCA [Small Business Community Association] Business Persons of the Year recipients. We won a lot of awards for our work. Over the course of time, we realized that that stuff is really quite empty.

People saw that we were leading our business in a very fundamentally different way. The first thing we [Brett and I] did in writing our business plan was to each independently document our core values. Then we reconciled our values with one another. Our values statement became the basis for everything we do.

"Our values statement became the basis for everything we do."

[The values have] evolved in the words but they are fundamentally the same. Our core values were the things that everyone was seeing as unique and powerful—which were that if we put people first, everything else will follow. Success will follow if we put people at the center of how we approach our work. Because of our values, people became very attracted and magnetized to our work and the company we had created—our philosophy on how we ran our business.

We have been in and out of living our core values; but when we're living them, it seems like success is easy. And when we start to deviate from that, things start to get really rocky. Going back to our core values statement has been the reason for our success.

Our values revolve around integrity first—do what you say you are going to do. Autonomy—we don't babysit; and if you require that, you don't belong here. Show up and be part of the family—at the end of the day, have each other's backs.

If you can't operate that way and you're here to create division or tension, you gossip, you're a trouble-maker, then you are not invited to stay. We've created an environment that has a healthy set of behaviors that are based upon trust, direct communication, supporting one another, and healthy conflict.

Good people [can] go bad. If they do that and show their true colors, they need to go before they become a bad influence and negatively affect the culture. I have accepted that it's part of the equation. I have had to get past taking it personally. I now recognize this is just business, and it happens.

I mentor about 20 of our folks here. I have very direct, fierce conversations with them about where they're at and what it's going to take for them to be successful here on an ongoing basis.

Values are your guide for weathering ethical dilemmas. They become the fabric for weaving good sound decisions. Values become your employees' moral compass. For your company's values to permeate throughout your organization, it will take conscious, consistent, deliberate actions.

"Values are your guide for weathering ethical dilemmas. They become the fabric for weaving good sound decisions."

Margie went on to describe how they are consciously creating culture.

In the very beginning, culture was at the center of what we do. Three to four years into our business, we created something called our "Culture Club." It's all about being deliberate and intentional with culture. Our company participates in organizing 10 to 12 events per year that are designed specifically to support our culture in order for us to stay connected to each other, to play, to challenge one another. That thing really lives on its own now. It used to be that I had to drive it. Now the employees drive it. We've put mechanisms in place, like if you are new to the company, you immediately get involved in this. That's the best way to get your arms around what we are. The company organizes all these events—not just one group of people. Everyone in the company gets assigned to certain events, so we all have a stake in the game to make these things really good. Almost every month we have something we come together on. You have to be deliberate on that stuff, or it just doesn't happen.

Success to me is having an engaged team that does great work and wants to stay here.

If you're happy and you're fulfilled by your work, you're going to do better work. You're going to continue to want to create great results so that you continue to get the same type of feedback and encouragement and opportunities. It feeds on itself.

---

*"Success to me is having an engaged team
that does great work and wants to stay here."*

Margie and Brett have created a high-tech company with heart and spirit where strong core values are part of the fabric of their culture. Here are the values Sitewire's people stand for:

Empathy: *Being humble and understanding of others enables us to design better experiences for everyone.*

Audacity: *We are bold, passionate, and ambitious when it comes to our work and the outcomes we create for others.*

Curiosity: *Childlike curiosity fueled by love for discovery and exploration are the keys to continuous innovation.*

Happiness: *Making time for play and rest restores our creative energy and enriches our work together.*

Collaboration: *Flexible, cross-discipline teams can achieve more together than any one of us could on our own.*

Simplicity: *Find simplicity in the complex and pursue clarity, consistency, and balance in everything.*

At TLC, we have persisted through many situations by staying true to our values. We strive to exemplify the following core values:

Well-Engineered Processes – *Our custom-designed group facilitations, training, coaching, and speaking experiences are creative, organized, holistic, thoughtful, and expertly led by our competent professionals to meet the specific needs of each client we serve.*

Inspiring Experiences and Resources – *We are enthusiastic and optimistic about our message and design all our group and individual experiences to be uplifting, engaging, encouraging, and fun.*

Lasting Relationships – *We strive to establish long-term trusting relationships with our clients by delivering exemplary service, remembering always to treat our customers and each other the way we want to be treated—with integrity, respect, honesty, empathy, and compassion.*

Purposeful Communication – *We understand the importance of good, quality communication for effective learning. We design our dynamic presentations, classes, and coaching sessions to meet the diverse learning styles and preferences of our audiences—incorporating visual, auditory, kinesthetic, creative and analytical elements to convey our message.*

Core values form the root system of your organization. Values nourish and stabilize your company. They represent the ideals that your organization stands for. They form your legacy. The more widespread and deeply imbedded your values, the more likely it is that your organization will stand the test of time. A company that knows and practices core values can weather storms and the winds of change.

A company with a clearly defined and well-lived value system is a harmonious, happy place to work. Values should be at the core of all the decisions employees make. They form the culture of the organization. Your shared values will become what your company stands for.

---

*"Values should be at the core
of all the decisions employees make."*

To have your company's values come alive, they need to be reinforced in every process and at every opportunity. They will have to be nurtured until they germinate and sprout in every business decision your employees make.

Strengthening values is like lifting weights to strengthen your muscles; it takes continuous practice and repetition before you begin to see lasting, positive results. So be diligent. Be patient.

Don't hire warm bodies who possess just the knowledge and skills you are looking for, but be sure they demonstrate the values and behaviors you are looking for. Values are difficult to teach to someone who doesn't see them as important.

Reward people for living your company values. Take corrective action when they don't. Release people who continually, consciously compromise your values.

So why do values matter so much? They create a magnetic, attractive energy, attracting the right people to work in your company and attracting the right customers to purchase your products and services.

Core Values are the behaviors that are expected from everyone in your company—top to bottom, with no exceptions. They answer these questions: "How do you choose to be? How do you want to be treated? What do you choose to stand for?"

To facilitate the discovery of your organization's Core Values, refer to the **Step-by-Step Facilitator's Guide** in the last section of the book.

Energizing Thoughts to Ponder
for Chapter 3

1. What do you want your company to stand for?

2. How do you want your employees to treat each other?

3. How do you want your employees to treat your customers?

4. What do you want your legacy to be?

Chapter 4

Know Your Business

*"When you discover your mission, you will feel its demand.
It will fill you with enthusiasm and a burning desire
to get to work on it."*

~W. Clement Stone

Businessman, philanthropist, and self-help author

What's the business you're in—or about?

Once you have created your mission statement, you will have defined the limits of what you will focus on as an organization. It is a valuable tool to decide on what to expend precious resources.

Recently, I enjoyed facilitating a strategic planning process with one of my clients, Arizona Cooperative Therapies (ACT). They have assembled an amazing cooperative of therapy provider developmental specialists for young children and their families. Here's their success story about the power of having a clear mission that everyone has bought into and supports, as told by one of the founding members, Leo Huppert.

> *An Arizona Early Intervention Program (AzEIP) contract was going to be coming about in 2006, and the State was not looking for small providers because of the scale of the contract.*
>
> *There were three of us who were good friends, small providers. We started talking about what we could do.*
>
> *We didn't know a lot about co-ops [cooperatives], but we started talking with the State of Arizona and a person from the Federated Human Services Cooperative that worked on the family side with kids with disabilities. They hooked us up with an attorney in Colorado who was an expert in Co-ops. The important thing for us is that we wanted to remain small business owners; but at the same time we wanted to pull together to do bigger projects.*

Originally the founders of ACT had a limited focus of being awarded one or several of the upcoming State contracts.

> *Our first focus was the State contract, but our attorney kept beating into us. When we shared our limited idea, our co-op attorney responded forcefully, "Don't do that! You guys can do so many things as a co-op. Don't limit yourselves!" So he's the one who steered us toward the bigger picture when we were defining our mission for the bylaws. We realized that we needed to diversify and do some other things because we really could as a co-op. We have that authority.*
>
> *We five knew it would work because we were all small businesses. We were independent to a point; but at the same time we also understood that we had to work together if we wanted to do bigger things. That's the benefit of being in the co-op. Everybody has everybody's back.*

"Once you have created your mission statement, you will have defined the limits of what you will focus on as an organization."

The Arizona Cooperative Therapies (ACT) organization was born. Their purpose in coming together was to *"provide opportunities for agencies to succeed through collaboration."*

The original and primary mission of the Co-op was *"to enable its members to provide therapy and support services in the State of Arizona. Co-operative philosophy and values are an essential part of the Co-op's enterprise; therefore, the Co-op will give equitable consideration to the various abilities of its members to provide services through the Co-op."*

In essence, the Co-op was formed to win large contracts, share resources, and funnel clients and income to its member agencies so that all could prosper.

The Co-op began with five member agencies. Many others watched and waited to see if the Co-op could indeed succeed in securing the upcoming contract.

ACT's membership continued to grow as they built relationships and shared information and possibilities with each other and the agencies which would eventually administer the contract. Six years after the initial idea and the crafting of their mission, they responded to the state's request for proposals. So how did they do, you ask?

> We were putting in for all nine regions [in the Phoenix Metropolitan Area], but we didn't know what we would get. A lot of people were really going on faith that, hopefully, we would get a contract for their specific region.
>
> We asked ourselves, "From an administrative standpoint, what if we get all nine regions, how are we going to handle that?" We're going from running our own small companies to running this large organization.
>
> Then the announcement came.
>
> Around Thanksgiving in 2012, I was at Kristin's (one of the Co-op members) office—that she shared with her husband's dental office—up on a ladder decorating for the holidays when the announcement came out. . . . Kristin took the call and shouted up to me, "You're not going to believe this. We got all nine regions!"
>
> I was already thinking, "How are we going to do this?"
>
> She said, "Wow! How come you're not that excited?"

I was excited and overwhelmed at the same time. And then she added, "Oh, by the way, the contract starts February 1, 2013."

The State awarded ACT all nine regions because we were one of the top performers on the RFP. They definitely saw us as the most qualified. And the State said that they really liked the idea of a cooperative. I think the State understood the cooperative idea better even than the providers did.

The leaders were elated and, at the same time, overwhelmed. They quickly went to work building and training their support staff, recruiting and training more agencies to serve the families and each region, and putting in place the necessary systems and procedures. It was an intense amount of work to get the project up and running, and then to have to wait months to see any money from the contract. The founders were acting purely on faith. Many had to borrow from their own businesses, friends, and families; some mortgaged their homes, and others maxed out their credit limits. A lot of soul searching ensued. "Can we really do this? How much longer can we hang on before we start seeing income?" 2013 was hell! In fact, some of the original founders bailed out before seeing a dime. Leo reminisced about that awkward time.

It was exciting but at the same time worrisome. That first couple of months we were thinking, "Oh, my gosh, what have we gotten ourselves into?"

We stuck with it because of the kids. Because of the work we do. We all said, "If we were in any other business, no one would have stayed."

To help solve contract payment issues with the State agencies, ACT even reached out to other contract providers in the State and formed a provider group to help streamline the contract systems and processes and support each other. In essence, they formed a collaborative with their competitors so that everyone could win. After all, their mission was, and still is, all about collaborating with agencies. When was the last time you saw that in business?

The co-op turned the corner in 2014. Money began flowing to the providers. They took a collective deep breath, regrouped, and refreshed their mission. I had the privilege of guiding the ACT leaders through the strategic planning process as they set their sights on a bigger picture. Leo said…

ACT did not have a strategic plan at the start. We realized that we needed to get better organized. After going through the strategic planning process, people see we have a vision. They work better together. I think that, early on, even though people were working together, it was more about survival. Now it's more about, "Okay, this is the benefit I see in working together." The strategic planning gave us a focus.

Their new mission has expanded the entire organization's thinking:

Through collaboration with our early childhood provider agencies, we uphold exceptional standards of practice and business ethics for family-centered services in Arizona.

To bring their mission to full fruition, work groups were established to involve more members in leading *their* organizations. We collaboratively developed a leadership training program to strengthen the ACT culture and fulfill the co-op's mission.

Culture is really important. The culture is the foundation for this, because if you have a culture of working together and supporting each other, then it's going to make your problems feel a lot less onerous. It's like a relief, in a way, because you know there are other people there to help get you through that.

"If you have a culture of working together and supporting each other, then it's going to make your problems feel a lot less onerous."

ACT is now thriving. Are there still issues? Sure! But the Co-op members function with a higher level of clarity. Everyone has a greater understanding of ACT's culture and direction, and they are even having more fun! Leo sums it up this way:

*The fun part is when you do get to celebrate, you get to celebrate as a group. "Hey you know what? We did this! We did this as a group together. It's not about **me** or I, it's about how **we** all came together to make this work."*

The ACT organization has demonstrated the power that a clear mission can have on everyone involved in the organization and the clients they serve.

Do you have a mission statement that clearly defines the unique business that you are in or about? Do your employees and customers understand your organization's mission?

Clearly defining your mission helps you to know which opportunities to say 'yes' to and which to turn down. It becomes a major component of your "Cone of Influence." It becomes your "energy umbrella." Every opportunity under the umbrella of your mission is a wise investment of your organization's energy and resources. Anything outside the umbrella will not resonate with what is important to your organization.

"Clearly defining your mission helps you to know what opportunities to say 'yes' to and which to turn down."

I always recommend to my clients that they revisit their mission, because their organization needs to evolve as the needs of their target market changes. Your organization's core purpose and core values should stand the test of time once you get them right. However, keep your mission like clay that you continue to mold as you get clearer on the business you're in or about.

"Keep your mission like clay that you continue to mold as you get clearer on the business you're in or about."

A mission statement is an umbrella proposition that should encompass all you chose to do. It defines the business you are in or about. A mission statement, well written, will answer the following questions:

1. *How do you choose to have people behave (most important core values)?*

2. *Why is your organization here (core purpose; the heart of your mission statement)?*

3. *What does your organization do (products and services you provide)?*

4. *What results do you desire for your organization (beyond just making money)?*

5. *Who does your organization serve (your customers)?*

The key to crafting a good mission statement is to make it simple but not too vague. Make it heartfelt and not too heady. Make it unique to your organization so as to distinguish you from your competitors. Make it memorable and inspiring to all who read it.

Here are a few more mission statement examples that may help get you started with creating your own:

Starbucks Mission: *To inspire and nurture the human spirit—one person, one cup, and one neighborhood at a time.*

Our TLC Mission: *We help create cultures of character and success that inspire hope and awaken the greatness in people, organizations and communities—guiding organizations to get clear, get organized, get going, and get results.*

When you have completed your organizational mission statement, consider asking your department managers to gather with their direct reports to craft each department's mission statement. This exercise will help employees to become clearer about the scope of their service to the organization. Additionally, you will find it to be a meaningful and engaging employee team building experience.

To facilitate your own mission statement process, see the **Step-by-Step Facilitator's Guide** in the last section of the book.

Energizing Thoughts to Ponder
for Chapter 4

1. What does your organization do (products and services you provide)?

2. What results do you desire for your organization (beyond just making money)?

3. Who does your organization serve (your customers)?

4. How do you define the business you're in or about?

Chapter 5

Envision Your Future

"If you can dream it, you can do it."

~Walt Disney

Entrepreneur and creator of "The happiest place on earth"

When you create a clear vision, it expands the collective thinking of your organization to encompass greater possibility and influence. A lofty vision is energizing. It excites everyone involved. It generates hope for the future.

What do you see as your organization's most desirable future state—with everything in perfect working order? Don't worry about when you will achieve it; instead, focus your energy first on *what it looks like*. Then, after you've created the perfect picture, by all means begin identifying the timeframes in which you think you can achieve each of the elements of the vision.

"When you create a clear vision, it expands the collective thinking of your organization to encompass greater possibility and influence."

As a personal practice, I make it a point to do business with people who create an extraordinary experience. One such company is T.C. Eggington's in Mesa, Arizona—my favorite brunch destination. There is something very special about this multi-award-winning, 30-year-old Best of Phoenix eating establishment.

Recently, Thom Coker (owner and founder) and I fondly reminisced about watching each others' families grow from babies into adults during those years. I thought about the many casual business meetings I enjoyed at his restaurant, the fun times I spent celebrating with family and friends, and the books—like this one—that I felt inspired to write while enjoying breakfast there.

Whenever I have been in the vicinity, I have always felt a strong pull to return to "my home away from home." So, what's the attraction? It's not just the food, which is 'egg-ceptional' (a little egg pun) but also the inviting atmosphere and the friendly treatment I receive as a valued customer.

Recently, I asked Thom, "How do you do it? How do you provide this exceptional award-winning experience day-in and day-out?"

"I hire the right people, folks who are passionate about our vision," Thom replied. Then he handed me a rack card with this vivid vision displayed on one side…

T.C. Eggington's Brunchery…
What a Difference!

An exciting opportunity to enjoy an extra special eating experience for young and old alike. Whether over friendly light conversation of business that starts with the "Crack O' Dawn," T.C. Eggington's is a delicious way to start your day.

Our original recipes are prepared from scratch every day with only the freshest ingredients. Cooked to your order exclusively in our kitchen for your pleasure, and served up with style. T.C. Eggington's is as fresh as a smile, warm and homelike.

Fascinations of flavors. Abundant aromas. And creative cooking creations, all brought to you hearty and home made. Let your taste buds take charge of your imagination—the smells of a big fresh breakfast come wafting out of an Olde English country kitchen.

T.C. Eggington's is a concept so unique, so satisfying, so original you just can't wait to tell your friends. As you begin to describe your fun-filled food experience, you'll suddenly recall everyone else's platefuls of open-faced sandwiches, plentiful colorful salads, skillet dishes and frittatas were so irresistible…

You'll also remember the fun fresh approach to service, and their genuine desire to make you feel special. You just know they're personally involved and want to do everything exactly right. Yes, T.C. Eggington's touch of casual sophistication is exceeded only by the quality and value of its excellent food.

Alas…if you were an egg, wouldn't "you" want to be cracked up to T.C. Eggington's high standards?

When I read Thom's vision, I said to myself, "That's it! That's what I experience every time I'm here." I can imagine that as you read their vision, you also felt a pull to experience this special place.

Thom trains and mentors his employees to do their parts to make Eggington's vision a reality for each customer.

Whether you are leading a company or a community, it is important to involve everyone in the visioning process so as to create enthusiastic buy-in, support, and a sense of personal 'ownership' from your employees. After all, aren't your employees the ones who are in the best position to bring it to life?

A long-standing client of mine has taken the visioning process to the highest level of community involvement I have experienced in my twenty-five years as a facilitator. It has paid big dividends for the Salt River Pima-Maricopa Indian Community (SRPMIC), a very progressive and savvy Indian tribe, located in Scottsdale, Arizona.

Recently, I had the chance to reflect on SRPMIC's visioning and planning efforts with the tribe's Community Manager, Bryan Meyers, who has been in that position for 17 years. One of their recent success stories is unprecedented in Native American communities. Here's how he describes it:

> In the late 80s SRPMIC began visioning through public involvement. People weren't used to the term "vision" back then, so we labeled it a "public involvement" process. What drove that process was the announcement of a freeway that was to pass through SRPMIC land—the Pima Commercial Corridor was born.
>
> We hired an architectural firm to come in and lead a bunch of public meetings. It was really a "visioning" process. It was the beginning of the Community really doing that type of process. A lot of it was set on what they wanted to see in the future in various areas as well as physical space areas but also about what is important to them—their environment and their culture.
>
> People appreciated the process. Our Community Members are very connected with the land and each other and really want to have their wants and desires to be heard. They like to participate actively in governance and visioning. When you go through those types of processes, if they're done right, it creates experiences that are way more valuable and lasting than just the document that gets put on the shelf. Once you hear it and you're involved in it and you create that experience and you buy in to it, it becomes part of your being, your understanding of where people want to go—putting yourself in their perspective.

That's the power of employee or member engagement. It creates a deep level of understanding and empathy for peoples' desires and expectations. Bryan continued,

> The vision, mission and core values have bridged four to five different leadership Councils. That's one really

unique thing about the Community—and even if you look at that first work that was done with visioning, there are a lot of common threads in there especially from the vision perspective.

Some parts of the vision are principles that are so imbedded in the culture that I don't think we'll see big changes [from the next generation of leaders]. There may be some priority shifts and differences, but I really don't envision much movement in the overall direction of the vision.

When we involve our Community Members in visioning they see it as "you reached out, you listened," especially when they see things happening that match what they said or their direction. People feel like they're invested when they come out to participate. If they don't see anything happening for long periods of time, that's not helpful across the board for many reasons. I think that's probably why, for the most part, our elected officials have stayed in tenure for long periods of time because they've been good about listening at the meetings to what the Community as a whole wants.

Our visioning processes and strategic planning have enabled us to be more nimble and make quicker decisions when we see an opportunity that you know aligns with our direction. We refer to our vision and plan often. It gives people confidence that we're not just plucking stuff out of the air. There's a thought-out, logical process that we're following; and it's consistent.

"Our visioning processes and strategic planning have enabled us to be more nimble and make quicker decisions."

Here's a great example of how, because of their clear vision and well-thought-out strategic plan, SRPMIC was prepared to seize a huge, high-value, high-risk opportunity. It required them to make a quick decision or lose the opportunity forever. Bryan shared how this colossal project unfolded.

In 2009, I was approached initially by a developer who was one of our commercial tenants on the Pima Corridor. He told me that the Arizona Diamondbacks and Colorado Rockies were interested in relocating their spring training facility from Tucson to the Phoenix area and that they wanted to know if we would be interested. At the time, we were unaware that they had already advertised an RFP for it.

It was a big deal for us when it was first brought up as a concept. My initial reaction was that this would be hard to convince people to do. We were just at a difficult time because the economy had really dipped, but the more I thought about it, the more I started to buy into it. Our Treasurer at the time also started getting buy-in for the idea. We asked ourselves, "Is this really what we need?"

There are infinite opportunities out there in which an organization can invest its valuable resources. Bryan asked a great question when this opportunity presented itself. In essence, he was asking if it was relevant to SRPMIC's purpose, values, mission, vision, and goals. Because the Community already had clarity around those elements, they knew it resonated. Coincidentally, my colleague, Perci Ami (I call her the happy Hopi), and I had guided them through an update to their strategic plan that year. So their direction was fresh and crystal clear. Bryan shared how things unfolded.

Through our visioning and strategic planning efforts we already had planned developing entertainment venues on that Corridor, so we saw its value even though we knew that it could be politically a little bit risky—that the people might not have the same level of vision that we had. We believed that it would help stimulate our economy, and we felt it [would] complement [other entertainment businesses] that we already had in place. It would surely put us on the map as being credible to work with—and that was another thing I thought would be important. If there were doubters out there (other developers), everything ranging from large boxes to small restaurants or hotels, we felt sure this project would have such a high profile that if these two major sports teams put their faith in us, we could pull it off and it would be the catalyst for other future projects. It was very intentional how we did it.

We very much saw it as a catalyst across many areas. We thought about the fact that when most people were shutting down their construction projects, this development would be an opportunity to take advantage of low construction costs because we thought we could get some good numbers on getting it built. It would certainly provide a lot of job opportunities. We believed we could leverage a number of related Community businesses into becoming direct vendors to the project, so it was kind of our own version of what the federal government did a little bit later for the larger economy—trying to push and infuse their own funds in to help kick-start the national economy. We felt it was going to be really important to catch the next wave when the economy came out of the trench and people started building again.

It turns out that when the economy did begin recovering, we were on the cusp of having a few new developments already on the drawing board.

Having already created our vision and strategic plan helped. You never know what opportunities may come your way. The key is to be ready and flexible when they do. So, if we hadn't done any of the visioning and planning, I'm not sure we could have pulled off that Spring Training project. Because we had been talking about our vision frequently, the Council was ready. They understood the importance, they understood the linkage; it's like building trust—it doesn't happen overnight. It doesn't happen after one PowerPoint presentation. It's sometimes a matter of years of consistent messaging, talking, agreeing, and consensus-building on what's important.

A lot of people said we couldn't do it. Ironically, I don't know if we were just naive, but there was never a doubt in my mind; it was just not optional for it not to work. We had to have it open by Spring Training. Of course, we can do *it! Now we can say, "Hey! Yeah, we're an Indian tribe, but these guys know what they're doing. . . look at what we could do together!"*

We did it! We were awarded the contract in 2009. The first Spring Training season was in 2011. We built the entire project in about 14 months! On time for opening day!

"You never know what opportunities may come your way. The key is to be ready and flexible when they do."

SRPMIC leadership's assessment of the merits of constructing the first professional Spring Training facility on Indian land proved true. It put SRPMIC on the map. Salt River Fields has won virtually every award there is to win. For every one of the past five years, it has been ranked as a *Class A* American sports-related venue—even ahead of the new Dallas Cowboys stadium. SRPMIC indeed did, and still is, "riding the next wave." Because of Salt River Fields, the Pima Entertainment Corridor has been a magnet, an anchor, and bridge for bringing other businesses to the Community. During Spring Training, revenues significantly spike for other entertainment, shopping centers, and hospitality businesses on SRPMIC land. It's undeniable, even to the naysayers, that Salt River Fields has been the catalyst for increasing SRPMIC revenues. Bryan has had fun hearing what people are saying now.

I've heard tons of people talking about our Spring Training facility. It's funny, even on airplanes I never say anything to anybody. I always just sit in the back listening. It's fascinating that I've been on two trips recently, and it happened to be around Spring Training, so people were traveling for that reason; and it makes me feel good when I'm on a plane, and I overhear conversations, "Hey, if you're coming to Phoenix, you should go to a Spring Training game, and make sure you go to Salt River Fields; and also make sure you go to the Orange Sky (a high-end SRPMIC casino restaurant), or make sure you go to this or that."

It's fascinating . . . I'll get in trouble because my wife will elbow me when they starting quoting things that are not correct and I think she wants me to correct them; but I fight the urge and just let it go.

The SRPMIC leaders had the courage to take a big risk to bring their vision alive. The results have been astounding. Visioning and Community Member involvement is a vital continuing process for the SRPMIC. The following is the overreaching vision that continues to guide SRPMIC leaders in making decisions in the best interest of their Community.

The Vision of the SRPMIC

Acknowledging our Creator is essential to the vision of the Salt River Pima-Maricopa Indian Community to improve and preserve the quality of life for our people, the Onk Akimel O'Odham and Xalychidom Piipaash.

We embrace the spirit of our ancestors, elders' wisdom, and create a legacy of honor, pride and respect for our future generations. This vision includes the preservation of the values of our culture and traditions.

Our commitment includes:

- *Protecting the lands and our people*
- *Preservation and sustainability of the land and environmental balance*
- *Embracing sovereignty as our inherent right*
- *A spiritually, mentally, emotionally and physically healthy life-style*
- *A dedication to education*
- *Promoting well-planned economic growth to insure financial security*

The SRPMIC vision statement is a snapshot of the desired future state of their Community. Imbedded within the vision are several cultural values important to the happiness and success of past, present and future generations—wisdom, honor, pride, and respect.

*"Visioning and Community Member involvement
is a vital, continuing process."*

In 2010, my associate, Perci, and I had the honor to facilitate SRPMIC's vision process. It is our hope that creating this next generation Vision 20/20 document will help create a common thread of Community Member priorities for the long-term success of the Community, even as changes in leadership occur.

One of the SRPMIC Council Members said this about the importance of vision: *"We have to deal with change constantly; like every other government, you can't stay in the same place if it doesn't fit anymore. It has always been of value to know what the people think, and what the people want. You look at the Vision and see what the people said; it gives you guidance and helps shape direction on future issues and projects such as transportation, land use, and tribal government."*

Bryan Meyers said, *"The SRPMIC Council thought it would be a good idea to update the vision document and use the process as an opportunity to reach out to the constituency, the Membership, to get their input to help guide the Community in the future for developing policies and actions or projects to make sure all government and Community activities are synchronized with the new vision."*

The Vision 20/20 facilitated process was designed to gather Community Member comments and concerns in a reasonable period of time. The Community-wide effort accomplished the following objectives:

- Gathered significant Community Member input and buy-in for the future of the SRPMIC, providing guidance from the people

- Became a reference guide for SRPMIC Community Councils for the next decade

- Provided SRPMIC staff with high-level direction from Council

- Provided a reference document for anyone who needs to refer to it

- Developed the focus for setting policies and direction for present and future Councils and staff

Over the course of several months, from June to August of 2010, eighteen forums were held in which Community Member facilitators—that we trained—gathered Community Member input.

The process was specifically designed such that everyone (youth, adults, seniors) had the opportunity to be heard. Neutral facilitators gently guided the participants toward sharing their ideas, which were captured in their own words.

It is fun and energizing to imagine what is possible when you embark on a visioning process that involves everyone in your organization or community. I love this part of the strategic planning process. It's like taking out your crystal ball. It's about seeing what's possible for your company and everyone in it. It is a great time to let your creative juices flow.

"It is fun and energizing to imagine what is possible when you embark on a visioning process that involves your organization or community."

What do you see (your vision) for your company in its desired future state? If everything were humming along perfectly, what would it look like? What's happening with customers? What's happening with staff? What systems are in place? What's happening financially? What difference are you making in your community—in the world?

What is the highest you can aspire to as a company? What can you be the best at in the world?

These are just some of the questions to consider. Whatever questions you choose to ask your employees or members, they will come away inspired and hopeful of their future with your organization.

Some companies create simple vision statements. Some develop more elaborate descriptions. There is no magic formula about what the final form should look like. My preference is to guide companies to create as much detail as possible so that they create a clear, vivid picture of what they desire for the organization in its ideal future state. Then, with that picture in mind, they can create an overreaching statement that encapsulates the vision.

At TLC, we have created such an overreaching vision statement.

TLC Vision – *We are the best at providing transformational success services to enlightened leaders who aspire to make a lasting, positive difference in the world.*

Some of my clients have also created a more detailed *Credo* (a statement of beliefs) to capture their picture of what their organization looks like in perfect working order. See Appendix D for an example of a Credo created by Lynn Kusy while he was Executive Director of the Phoenix-Mesa Gateway Airport Authority.

For tips on how to facilitate your own visioning process, see the **Step-by-Step Facilitator's Guide** in the last section of the book.

Energizing Thoughts to Ponder
for Chapter 5

1. What do you envision for your company operating in perfect working order?

2. What can you be the best at in the world?

3. What is the biggest difference your organization can make in the world?

2nd Phase: Get Organized

"First comes the thought, then organization of that thought into ideas and plans, then transformation of those plans into reality."

~Napoleon Hill
Author, *Law of Success*

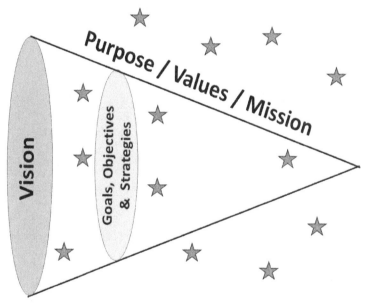

Figure 6A: The Cone of Influence (Get Organized)

Now that you've gotten clear, it's time to get organized and align your attention with your intentions.

In the previous chapters, you set the direction of your organization by defining your core purpose, core values, mission, and vision. Consequently, you created the boundaries of your Cone of Influence. Now you are ready to set relevant goals, objectives, and strategies that align with your organization's direction. Again, the stars within the boundaries of the Cone of Influence are potential opportunities to use when setting your goals.

That's the essence of the 2nd Phase: "**Get Organized.**"

Chapter 6

Do Some Soul Searching

"In the business world, the rearview mirror is always clearer than the windshield."

~Warren Buffett
CEO, Berkshire Hathaway, and philanthropist

Before beginning any journey, you first need to know where you are.

Remember the last time you were planning a trip and consulted a map? First, you identified your current position. Next, you located your destination. And then you figured out the best route between the two points.

In a similar manner, applying the elements presented in this chapter will enable you first to understand your current position as an organization and then to chart the best course toward your goals and figure out the actions needed to reach your company's vision.

It's time to do some soul-searching. The deeper you choose to go into your analysis, the easier your next steps will be. Some facilitators call this next part of the process a SWOT analysis (Strengths, Weaknesses, Opportunities, and Threats). But I like to call upon a "higher source" by renaming this soul-searching aspect the **SPOC** analysis (Strengths, Possible Improvements, Opportunities, and Challenges). It may seem trivial, but I've always loved the logical- and positive-minded Mr. Spock, from "Star Trek," so I suppose this is a tribute to him. Rest in peace, legendary actor Leonard Nimoy. Thanks for the memorable v-shaped hand signal and the benevolent affirmation, "Live long and prosper."

"Live long and prosper."

So, what is the SPOC analysis; and why should you do it? In the process of building your business, the SPOC analysis offers a great, revealing way to assess where you are right now and then to scan the business environment in order to anticipate the possibilities that might present themselves on your journey toward achieving your mission and vision. It also identifies key areas that you may want to focus attention upon in the form of goals, objectives, or strategies. We'll discuss more about that later.

Are you ready? Here's how the **SPOC Analysis** process works:

1. Answer the question "What are your organization's **Strengths**?" These are the areas in which your organization does well, in which you excel. Capitalize on these strengths, and your organization will prosper, your teams will maximize their potential, and your employees will be productive and fulfilled.

2. Answer the question "What **Possible Improvements** would help your organization to be more successful?" These are areas in which you may presently be experiencing some deficiencies. Some people call these weaknesses. However, they may not be weaknesses at all. Instead, they may simply

be elements that are not important to the success of your organization. When guiding leaders through this segment of the SPOC analysis, I prefer to coach them to be proactive in identifying what needs to be improved in order to achieve their core purpose, core values, mission, and vision more quickly and effectively. These deficiencies act as speed bumps, slowing your progress. *Hint: Look back at the "flat spots" that appear on your Circle of Success assessment wheel from Chapter 1. These particular areas need some sort of improvement.*

3. Answer the question "What potential *Opportunities* could be seized to move your organization toward accomplishing its mission and vision?" These ideas are most likely untapped activities and projects, or knowledge and skill-building events. These opportunities are represented by those stars, discussed previously, that fall within your Cone of Influence. Taking advantage of these opportunities will accelerate your progress toward success.

4. Answer the question "What *Challenges* may need to be overcome?" Consider them as obstacles or roadblocks standing in the way of achieving success. These challenges could even be showstoppers for you and your company. Like water flowing along a rocky stream, you will need to find creative solutions in order to make your way over, around or through these obstacles in order to realize your mission and vision.

5. If they didn't surface when you were brainstorming the "Opportunities" and "Challenges," what *trends* are emerging in your industry?

Answers to these five questions will help you to identify goals, objectives and strategies on which to focus your organization's energy and attention.

For tips on how to facilitate your own SPOC Analysis, see the **Step-by-Step Facilitator's Guide** at the end of the book.

Energizing Thoughts to Ponder
for Chapter 6

1. What are your *Strengths* as an organization?

2. What are *Possible Improvements* in order for your organization to succeed?

3. What *Opportunities* could you pursue to accelerate your progress?

4. What are potential *Challenges* that may stand in your way toward achieving success?

5. What trends are emerging in your industry?

Chapter 7

Focus Your Energy

"Passion is energy. Feel the power that comes from focusing on what excites you."

~Oprah Winfrey
Television and Radio Personality, and Bold Entrepreneur

With a vast number of opportunities to consider for your organization, how do you choose the ones that are most likely to bring you success? You need a reliable method for determining which opportunities to focus on. Here's how to make decision-making easier: Focus your attention on your intention.

"Focus your attention on your intention."

Given that so many interests and choices always compete for your precious resources, how do you decide which are most important to you and your organization?

In my years of professional facilitation and personal experience, I have come to believe in the value and power of a universal principle that has helped me and my clients to make effective, timely decisions—when to say "yes" to an opportunity and when to say "no".

This universal principle—called the Law of Attraction—states that whatever we focus our attention on gains strength and attracts more of the same. It is perhaps the most consistent and visible demonstration of the Law of Cause and Effect.

What you focus on expands and grows stronger. So why not focus upon what you *want*, rather than upon what you don't want? When you focus your attention (thoughts and actions) upon your intention (mission, vision, values, etc.), you send a clear message about what's important to you and your organization.

"What you focus on expands and grows stronger."

If you have ever seen the movie *Patch Adams*—based on a true story—you will remember that Robin Williams, who played Patch, checked himself into a mental hospital in an attempt to escape his problems. As an orderly escorted Patch to the common area, a resident patient jumped in front of Patch, held up four fingers in front of his face, and excitedly asked, "How many? How many fingers?" Surprised, Patch responded quickly, "Four!" In disgust, the patient blurted, "IDIOT!" and ran off.

Eventually, Patch discovered that the patient was a brilliant scientist named Arthur Mendelson. In a subsequent scene, Patch entered Arthur's room and asked what the four fingers meant. Arthur asked Patch to hold up four fingers in front of his face. Then, Arthur asked again, "How many?" Patch again said, "Four." Then Arthur told Patch not to focus on the fingers—to look past the fingers. When Patch looked past his fingers, they appeared to be transparent; and he saw eight fingers. Patch said, "Eight!"

"That's right!" Arthur encouraged Patch. "Don't focus on the problem—focus on the *solution*."

"Don't focus on the problem—focus on the solution."

Applying Arthur's wisdom of focusing on solutions and goals, you will discover that problems don't appear so daunting. That's what goal-setting will do for you and your organization—it will cause you to focus on what you want and what is important and constructive.

By taking time to clarify your purpose, mission, values, and vision, you will form the Cone of Influence for your organization. Then, by setting goals in alignment with this Cone of Influence, you will move purposefully toward their realization and create a greater chance for employee fulfillment. All these elements, working together, will complete your picture of success.

Defining your unique Cone of Influence will make it clearer to you which opportunities (symbolized by the stars) to say "yes" to, and which ones to say "no" to. Opportunities *within* your "Cone" will be in alignment with what is important to you. For those opportunities that are outside your "Cone," you can quickly say "no" and avoid wasting your precious time, resources, and energy. It is all about making sure that, in each present moment—right now—you focus on what matters most to you.

To be successful as an organization make sure that everything you and your employees do is in alignment with what is most important to the organization—by "focusing your attention on your intention." (See Figure 6B on the next page.) This model is actually a simplified way of showing how all the elements of the strategic planning process unfold and support each other—all leading to the wisest use of each moment of 'now.'

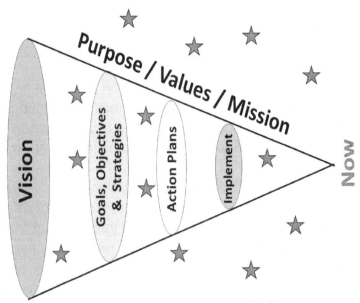

Figure 6B: Complete Cone of Influence

Here's how it works:

1. The Purpose, Values, Mission, and Vision form the "Cone of Influence" of your organization. These elements define the depth and breadth of what is important to your organization. The more lofty the Vision, the wider is the Cone of Influence.

2. The stars represent opportunities to expend or invest resources. Stars that are located outside the Cone of Influence represent opportunities to which you should say "no." They are not in alignment with the direction of your organization. Stars that appear within the Cone of Influence represent opportunities to which you could say "yes," depending on available resources. These are opportunities in alignment with what is important to your organization.

3. When Goals and Action Plans are developed for those opportunities within the Cone of Influence, they will help fulfill the Purpose, Mission, Values and Vision of your organization. Any pursuits of opportunities outside that realm will be wasted, scattered energy.

Thus far, you have defined the limits of the Cone of Influence. In the following chapters, you will focus your energy on developing Goals, Objectives, Strategies, and Action Plans—all in alignment with your culture and direction.

For tips on how to facilitate your own Cone of Influence discussion, see the **Step-by-Step Facilitator's Guide** at the end of the book.

Energizing Thoughts to Ponder
for Chapter 7

1. What opportunities are you saying "yes" to today that feel as though they may be taking you off course with regard to what is important to the success of your organization (i.e., not in alignment with your Purpose, Values, Mission, and Vision)?

2. What opportunities are presenting themselves today that seem to be in alignment with your organization's Purpose, Values, Mission, and Vision?

3. What possible opportunities are you considering that could be in alignment with what matters most to the success of your organization?

Chapter 8

Chart Your Course

"Goals provide the energy source that powers our lives. One of the best ways we can get the most from the energy we have is to focus it. That is what goals can do for us; concentrate our energy."

~Dennis Waitley
Author of 16 non-fiction books including *Seeds of Greatness*

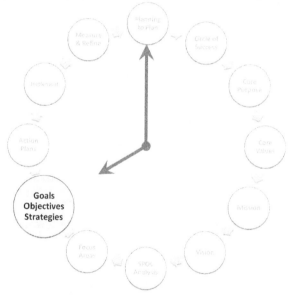

In Chapter 3, we discussed how Sitewire's founders created a powerful, value-rich culture at the inception of their company. Here's something unique and effective they do to involve everyone in establishing the direction of their company. Margie Traylor further elaborated on their story.

In the beginning, our annual strategic planning was more about numbers than strategy. It wasn't working. It wasn't good. It didn't really deliver results. We'd do the plan and then not do anything we said we'd do. It wasn't successful in any way, shape, or form.

Then, about five years ago, we began to look at planning again—but doing it differently. We needed to get out ahead of the curve. Accidentally, we had done well at getting ahead of the curve, but had not done it with purpose.

Then, my business partner, Brett, took the lead on strategic planning. He's a visionary. He's always out ahead of everything digital. We turned the corner on planning when we started planning from a market needs and visionary perspective versus a financial perspective.

Companies that use strategic planning to set only financial targets are missing out on some of the most rewarding benefits and possibilities. Sitewire leaders have taken strategic planning to the next level. You can, too.

"Companies that use strategic planning to set only financial targets are missing out on some of the most rewarding benefits and possibilities."

Our planning then became an exercise in identifying the trends in our industry and deciding what our business needs to do to support and take advantage of the trends. Of course, the financial piece came in to support that.

We've changed to shorter planning cycles—what we used to do annually we now do every two months because we're in such a rapidly evolving business.

*We took my business partner out of the day-to-day affairs of the company and, along with another big thinker in our organization, and allowed them **just to think**. Their primary job is to identify the highest and best use of our assets, to understand our customers' needs thoroughly, and to determine where the market and technology is going and, as a consequence, where our company needs to realign.*

My business partner is creating a strategic roadmap for us that we're executing . . . Our employees are actively involved in the planning process. They're able to identify upcoming trends in technology and make recommendations on things that we should try, to see if they're viable. They're helping seed ideas. If their ideas show viability, Bret starts to bake them into the strategic roadmap.

"Our employees are very involved in the planning process. They're able to identify upcoming trends ... and make recommendations on things that we should try, to see if they're viable."

Then, we take our top 20 employees (not necessarily in leadership roles) offsite and do strategic planning with them. That group is informed about the strategic vision and their unique roles in that two-month planning cycle. Their job is to set the course for their part of the business for the upcoming cycle and to be held accountable for their parts in it.

We have them come back at the end of the cycle and explain any successes or failures; and, based on what we learn, we re-set the roadmap for the next few months. Those 20 people are responsible for making their areas achieve those objectives for the period.

Eventually, every employee has a plan. The 20 come back with their own plans and, if they have people reporting to them, use their commitments to craft plans for their direct reports. We have just started having a company-wide meeting the same day they return from the bi-monthly sessions. Everyone hears right out of the gate what it is we've committed to for the next two months. Everyone has the chance to ask questions in real-time and buy into—or argue against—why the direction wasn't good.

Whenever we decide to repurpose our assets, we get the people affected involved; we include them in crafting the execution plan associated with the changes.

Once they see their role in it and see their future—using them as influencers—they do the heavy lifting within their departments to help people see the vision. It's not the talking heads that are doing it; it's the people in the business. That strategy works very well.

Involving all employees in the strategic planning process gives everyone a vested interest in the success of their organization. They feel a greater sense of ownership. Margie went on to say:

We don't get too far down the path before we get 20 other people involved in the vision. We don't go off and do a yearly plan and then come back and unload on people. As a result, most people don't feel like things are happening in a vacuum anymore; it's happening in a collaborative conversation. It's clear how we get things done now.

"We don't get too far down the path before we get 20 other people involved in the vision."

The strategic plan that you are developing will serve as your strategic roadmap, compass, and GPS for your business adventure.

On a side but related note, my wife, Lyn, and I love RVing. Whenever we're planning a trip, we first decide where we want to go. Then, we chart our course on a map to see what route we like best that will include other interesting destinations along the way. Then, we set goals or milestones for each day. Sometimes we choose the shortest distance from point "A" to point "B." At other times, we choose the most interesting and scenic routes, depending on our goals. We begin each day by programming our GPS with that day's destination (we affectionately call our GPS device Mrs. G). As a result of this guidance system in our truck, we receive continuous confirmation that we are on track and are not going astray. Yes, we begin with a plan; however, here's the beauty of our system: We build in flexibility for taking new and exciting excursions that we often times discover along the route.

Allowing for spontaneity, we have experienced some magical, enchanting adventures beyond our wildest dreams.

I suggest that you build in similar flexibility within the plan for your business. Allow it to unfold in new and exciting ways as you discover unknown vistas, as situations change, or when new trends emerge. Don't be so rigid that you miss valuable opportunities that present themselves along the way toward fulfilling your mission and vision.

Some strategic planning approaches make this part much too complicated. Again, just think of it like this: *Any Goals you set should be in alignment with your Purpose, Values, Mission, and Vision.*

A good initial question to ask is, "What themes or focus areas are most important to the success of our organization?" You may have already received clues to answer this question as you performed the Circle of Success Assessment and the SPOC (aka SWOT) analysis from Chapters 1 and 6, respectively.

Hint: Establish goals that will be inspiring and energizing, not just financial targets to achieve. Consider focus areas such as Employees, Products, Services, Outreach, and yes, of course, Financial. Adopt a holistic approach that will inspire your employees and increase the value you provide to your customers—the sum of which work together, contributing to your bottom line.

> *"Establish goals that will be inspiring and energizing, not just financial targets to achieve."*

Lofty goals can be both inspiring and daunting at the same time. With that in mind, you've probably heard the question, "How do you eat an elephant?" And you probably remember the answer: "One bite at a time!" This is exactly how you can help reduce the overwhelmed feeling people may experience as they begin to tackle "big, hairy, audacious goals" (BHAG's), an acronym created by Jim Collins and Jerry Porras in their book, *Built to Last.*

Large goals need to be broken down into smaller, "bite-sized" milestones in order to get a better understanding of what it will take to achieve them. These milestones are sometimes referred to as objectives, strategies and tactics. A goal can be segmented into objectives, objectives segmented into strategies, and strategies segmented into tactics—in a cascading effect, ranging from larger to smaller segments. This is similar to a stream cascading down a mountain. With each subsequent segment, the goal becomes more refined, more clear, and more specific.

Figure 7 shows a mindmap example of this cascading effect.

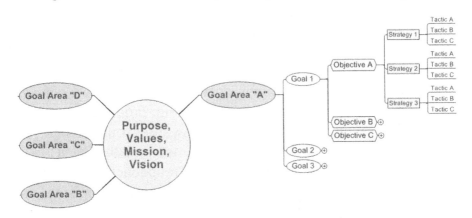

Figure 7: Mindmap of the cascading effect of strategic planning.

Once you have identified the Goal Areas, ask yourself, "Which Goals should we focus upon in order to improve or make strides in that area?"

Then ask, "What are major milestones that need to be achieved in order to accomplish each Goal?" These milestones become your "Objectives."

If your Objectives still seem daunting, ask yourself, "What needs to be done in order to accomplish these Objectives?" These milestones become your "Strategies."

Then, for each Strategy, ask yourself how you're going to do that. These strategies become your "Tactics," or action steps. (See the example on the next page.)

Example of the breakdown of a
Goal→Objective→Strategy→Tactic

Goal 1: By the end of the year, increase employee participation by 25 percent in the wellness program

> **<u>Objective A</u>:** By mid-year next year, increase employee registration by 15 percent for the weight loss challenge program
>
>> **<u>Strategy 1</u>:** Work with Department Managers to inform employees about the weight loss challenge program, this December 1
>>
>>> **<u>Tactic A</u>:** By this January 1, provide all Department Managers with a fact sheet about the weight loss challenge program to distribute to employees at weekly staff meetings

Here's a little guidance about setting goals the really S.M.A.R.T. W.A.Y. Make them...

- **Specific** (not too vague),

- **Measurable** (so you know the progress you're making),

- **Attainable** (but a definite stretch),

- **Relevant** (in alignment with your purpose, values, mission and vision), and...

- **Time-bound** (scheduled milestones). It is also important that you have them be...

- **Written** (this makes them more solid), and build in...

- **Accountability** (hence the need for individual development plans for your employees) and, finally, have a strong...

- **Yearning** to achieve them (never underestimate the power of enthusiasm).

On the next page is a real example of TLC Goal Areas and the cascading development of a Goal, Objectives, and Strategies.

Goals	Priority (A, B or C)
1. **Client Attraction**: Attract the right and perfect clients.	A
2. **Services Offered**: Offer services that are in high demand by our target audience.	A
3. **Product Development**: Offer products that are in high demand by our target audience.	A
4. **Professional Development**: Remain sharp and current by understanding the latest transformational learning developments.	B
5. **Personal Development**: Continue to grow, improve and re-energize as individuals.	B

Figure 8: Example of TLC Goal Areas and Goals

It has been my experience that the best way to begin identifying objectives and strategies is to create a mindmap for each goal. A mindmap is a powerful tool to see what is necessary to accomplish a goal. It really creates clarity and focus.

Writing this book was one of the objectives identified under this year's TLC Goal 3, Product Development. Figure 9 shows an example of a mindmap that I created even before I began writing this book.

Figure 9: Mindmap for Energize Your Business book

Think of goals more as a process than as a destination. People grow and become stronger as they stretch toward goals. The bigger and more hairy (difficult or complex) the goal, the greater is the potential for growth and transformation, so long as it doesn't cause people to feel too overwhelmed.

Enjoy this dynamic, effective process!

For tips on how to facilitate your own Goals, Objectives and Strategies session, see the **Step-by-Step Facilitator's Guide** in the last section of the book.

Energizing Thoughts to Ponder
for Chapter 8

1. What do you think are the most important themes or Focus Areas for your company?

2. What do you think are the Goals with the highest priorities to accomplish in each of those Focus Areas?

3. What are possible Objectives and Strategies that must be achieved in order to accomplish each of the Goals you have identified?

3rd Phase: Get Going

"William James said, 'When once a decision is reached and execution is the order of the day, dismiss absolutely all responsibility and care about the outcome.' He meant that once you have made a careful decision based on facts, go into action. Don't stop to reconsider. Don't begin to hesitate, worry and retrace your steps. Don't lose yourself in self-doubting which begets other doubts. Don't keep looking over your shoulder. There comes a time when any more investigation and thinking are harmful. There comes a time when we must decide and act and never look back."

~Dale Carnegie
Author, *How to Stop Worrying and Start Living*

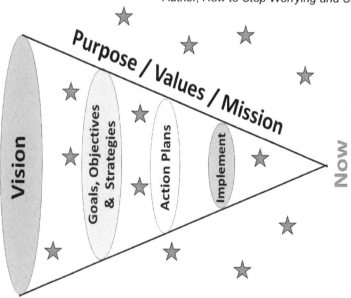

Figure 10: Cone of Influence (Get Going)

Now that you have a clear idea of the end results you want to see for the organization, it is time to map out and implement an action plan to get there.

As you and your employees implement the actions based upon your strategic plan, consider building in the important elements of accountability, assessment, and acknowledgment so you can stay on track and keep making progress. This section delves into possibilities for doing just that.

In order to realize optimal success, your ultimate goal is to focus everyone's attention upon the tasks necessary to implement the action plans.

Chapter 9

Prepare for Ignition

"When it comes to strategy, ponder less and do more."

~Jack Welch

Founder, Jack Welch Management Institute and
Former Chairman, General Electric Company

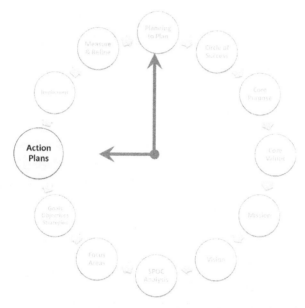

*"Remember, you and you alone are responsible for maintaining
your energy. Give up blaming, complaining, and excuse-making,
and keep taking action in the direction of your goals —
however mundane or lofty they may be."*

~Jack Canfield

Co-author, *The Success Principles* and
Chicken Soup for the Soul series

Me with Johnny "Cupcakes" Earle

It's important to pay attention to details. Such attention sends a signal to your employees and customers that you care. When something is out of place or out of character, people notice. Instead of your employees being bothered by these distractions, you want them to stay focused. Instead of your customers being distracted, you want them to be appreciative of the value they are receiving from your product or service.

After you have defined your Goals, Objectives and Strategies, it's time to identify how you are going to achieve them—tactically. It's time to pay attention to the details—to identify the detailed Tactics (action steps), to schedule the timeline for accomplishing them, to identify the resources required, and to assign people to each task. Now the proverbial "rubber meets the road." During the entire planning process, you have been building potential energy, similar to that of rollercoaster cars climbing the initial big hill. Now it's time for kinetic energy to take over as the rollercoaster cars rush down from the top of the hill—as you put your plans into action! It can be very exciting—and sometimes a little scary. So remember, too, that it's time to step into your fear and experience the fruits of your labor.

While writing this book, I attended a small business summit where I met a very creative, fearless, fun-loving, action-oriented, successful business owner named Johnny "Cupcakes" Earle. He's an energetic idea generator who demonstrates the power of making one's unique brand and ideas come alive through exciting, focused effort.

He started his company, Johnny Cupcakes, when he was only 19 years old without the support of money from investors. He earned his first million dollars when he was a mere 24 years old and, as a result, was featured in the *Wall Street Journal*.

Johnny's 14-year-old business is still thriving today because everything he has implemented has begun with a simple idea that he brought to life by springing into action before anyone else thought of it. Here's part of Johnny's zany story (for more of his story, go to www.JohnnyCupcakes.com).

I went to public schools. I had learning disabilities, and I had to be put in a charter school to learn at my own pace.

Growing up, I would see my parents spending so much time going to and from work; and they didn't spend too much time raising my little sister and me. So, at a young age, I was inspired to be an entrepreneur some day and figure out how I could spend more time with the people that I love.

I started 16 businesses before I was 16 years old. I sold lemonade, did garage sales, shoveled snow, illegally sold soda on the beach, did magic shows, worked in a record store, performed in a hardcore metal rock band, etc.. I became infatuated with the audience and creating a unique experience.

I like to say, "Do more of what makes you happy!" It's a simple phrase that you should always remember with this busy life that can sometimes get the best of you. It's really important to make time for those things you're passionate about.

"Do more of what makes you happy!"

I realized that I could do something I loved—something that makes other people happy—and I could figure out a way to get paid for this. It almost seems like magic in itself.

In high school, I decided to get an internship at a T-shirt company. Anytime a T-shirt came out of the printer, it was like an idea machine. And it inspired me.

People would call me all sorts of nicknames because my name was Johnny. "Johnny Cupcakes" came out of left field. I thought it was a funny nickname, so I put it on a T-shirt as a joke when I was getting T-shirts made for the hardcore metal band I used to be in. And I would wear them to work at the record store. And all these slumpy, miserable customers who would never make eye contact with me, they started laughing and saying, "What is that? What is Johnny Cupcakes? Is that a bakery? Is that an adult movie store?" I'm like, "No! No! It's just a T-shirt that I made." And these shirts made complete strangers smile and caused confusion. I like to trick people and make people happy.

As the result of these experiences, Johnny's inspired idea to start his own T-shirt company is now a reality.

I imagine that you have also had, or are having, an inspired idea to start your own business. Many people have ideas like this, but few act on them. Many let fear stop them. I have come to believe that the best way to dissipate fear is to brainstorm what it would take to make that idea a reality, and then quickly spring into some sort of action.

"The best way to dissipate fear is to brainstorm what it would take to make that idea a reality, and then quickly spring into some sort of action."

Here's how Johnny Cupcakes' business was born.

All of a sudden I found this new passion of mine— "Johnny Cupcakes"—advertising a bakery that didn't even exist. I began poking fun at pop culture, replacing pop icons with cupcakes.

All these tough guys used to come into my work with these skull and cross bones, and I'm like, "I'm going to put a cupcake there [instead of a skull]." Guys thought it was funny. Girls thought it was cute. It caused curiosity.

"Got cupcakes?" instead of "Got milk?"... Michael Jordan dunking a cupcake instead of a basketball. I even put these T-shirts into little tiny sneaker boxes to create the experience of opening shoes.

We even created a breakfast-themed T-shirt. We have customers that have camped out, sleeping on the street in front of my retail stores for up to two weeks to get some of these special-edition T-shirts.

We are always thinking, "What else can we do to get these people excited?"

I've met over 2,000 people who have my brand's logo tattooed on their body. If you do a Google search for "Johnny Cupcakes tattoos," you'll see some pretty crazy things. Some [of them] I'm not allowed to talk about. It was pretty freaky at first, but a lot of these customers have been inspired to start their own business or live a healthier lifestyle. [Johnny has never tasted alcohol or used drugs.]

We like to create experiences. Everything in the world has been done before. Nowadays, you cannot just come up with one or two things that make your company or your craft unique. You have to have at least a dozen things.

Over time, I've built up an amazing team—there are 35 of us now. I've learned to delegate. I learned I couldn't do it alone. It's your baby, but you have to learn to let go; or you're just going to keep treading water.

We've collaborated with other companies. We worked with Marilyn Monroe's estate, replacing her beauty mark with a tiny, tiny cupcake. We've done some stuff with Looney Tunes. Collaborations are great! The best thing you can get out of them is that cross-pollination—other people's customers and fans learning about your business and vice versa. Hello Kitty posted our shirt on their fan page. When we released this T-shirt, our website nearly crashed. We ended up making $250,000 in 24-hours with *zero traditional advertising. We couldn't believe this. We thought something was wrong with the website.*

That day, we realized the power of collaborations.

One of the most important lessons I've had to learn in my business is that I don't have to do it alone. I've also learned that I don't have to re-invent the wheel. In one of the previous chapters about creating a mission, you read that ACT formed an organization using the power of collaboration. Johnny has harnessed the same power. Here's more from Johnny about collaboration.

So, we decided to do it with the Ninja Turtles—to collaborate with them and make special-edition shirts. Making these shirts was a dream come true. We put our Johnny Cupcakes mark on all the graphic designs. Then, we asked ourselves, "What else could we do to make this special?" The Ninja Turtles themselves went out to our London shop on Carnegie Street to surprise the customers in line. All of the customers felt like a kid again. Some of them might even have gone to the bathroom in their pants.

Once you have an inspired idea or goal, ask yourself, "What else can I do to generate more energy around that idea?" When you are creating your action plans for your goals, brainstorm out-of-the-box ideas that can fully bring your idea to life. Here's Johnny in action again:

People have too many options. Why would they take a risk with you?

It's all about those experiences! Think outside the box to get people excited and passionate about supporting your ideas and your brand or your company.

"Think outside the box to get people excited and passionate about supporting your ideas and your brand or your company."

For "The Simpson's" anniversary several years ago, we packaged the T-shirts in oversized cupcake mix boxes.

Each box came with different items—socks, watch, bow tie, Itchy and Scratchy hat—all these things to create that experience. What could we do to push it further? A few things are not enough anymore. We decided to have an event at our stores. We gave out actual Duff energy drinks. We had real cupcake donuts made. We had Homer Simpson come out and strangle all our customers that were waiting in lines for T-shirts. My mother even dressed up as Marge Simpson and greeted everyone who came in to purchase T-shirts that day.

We even made actual movie trailers for every T-shirt design.

People thrive off of new experiences so much that they're willing to camp out for days. My concept is strange. But strange is good. Strange is important. It sets you apart from the rest.

We set up our stores to look and smell like bakeries. All my storefronts say "no sugar, no carbs, no fat, freshly baked." I purchase big deli refrigerators, big commercial ovens, a thousand-pound dough mixer that doesn't even work. We put our T-shirts in freezers. I even hide vanilla scented car deodorizers in my store, so when you walk in, you smell vanilla frosting. I even convinced a friend of mine that we mixed vanilla frosting in the paint, and I had him lick different sections of the wall. He really did this. Every day we trick people from around the world.

Inside the store, my ovens open and close at set times and steam jets out. We painted everything black and white so that what we're selling—our T-shirts—stands out. We laid out our floor tiles diagonally to make the small space appear larger. We also put giant mirrors on the walls to make the space appear larger. Employees have to walk through an oven (entrance to the stock room) to get your themed graphic shirt. And when you go to check out, there's a stove top with fake fire that flickers. There are fake pipes, fake frosting, fake sprinkles.

Always ask yourself, "What are twelve-plus things that make you unique?" And don't just stop there. Keep filling up your notebook with ideas, because the second you become comfortable is the moment another business is going to come in and steal your thunder.

"What are twelve-plus things that make you unique?"

Every time someone supports my brand, I want them to think it's their birthday. Often, I'll go into our warehouse and hand-write little personal notes on my customers' orders. It takes me two seconds to have a life-long customer. I encourage you to write handwritten notes. It goes a long way. It's a lost art. It's something that people don't usually forget. Thank your customers. Thank the people who support your brand. It's going to come right back around.

When you are identifying your actions, remember to build in ways to appreciate your customers and teams. American philosopher and psychologist William James once said, "The deepest principle in human nature is the craving to be appreciated."

As you are building your business, never lose sight of your "big why?" Remember how important it was to Johnny to spend time with his loved ones? As a result, he figured out how to weave it into his business plan.

One of the reasons I think I don't drink is that my dad was an alcoholic when I was growing up. He's actually been sober the past ten years. It's like I have a brand new dad. It's unbelievable! I'm so proud of my dad. I get to work with him. He's a carpenter. I get to hire him to work in our business—in our shops. I am so proud to work with my dad.

I was able to hire my mom full-time. I now get to see my mom every day. It's a true blessing. It's an indescribable experience getting to see my family all the time.

Remember, it's not about the money; it's about being happy doing what you love. If you can go to work every day laughing and smiling, that's a beautiful thing, because that affects every part of your life. Even if you're not yet financially successful, if you're doing what you love, the financial success will follow. Keep putting that hard work in and thinking differently.

Luck has nothing to do with it. If I can do this with learning difficulties, with something as bizarre as cupcakes on T-shirts, there is no reason whatsoever that you, with all of your resources and your network, can't come up with a more successful idea.

Stop making excuses, and start making stuff.

You have to have fun every day. You have to laugh.

I believe real success is being happy doing what you love.

"I believe real success is being happy doing what you love."

Johnny Cupcakes understands how to focus his attention on what matters most—what supports and energizes his brand. He is clear about when to say 'yes' and when to say 'no'.

At the heart of your branding are your purpose, values, mission, and vision. Your goals, objectives, strategies, and action plans are what bring it all to life.

Keep your eye on the prize—beyond making money. If you focus your attention on what matters most, the money will come.

"If you focus your attention on what matters most, the money will come."

It is always exciting when the fruits of your labor become visible. The company harvest represents goals achieved—success manifested. In the case of your company, a bountiful harvest serves your customers and employees.

In this chapter, you are preparing for ignition. You are going to divvy up all the pieces of the puzzle for the people in your organization to take action. Let everyone in your organization have a vested interest in accomplishing the goals. Include pieces of the goals in your employees' individual development plans.

Then coach them so that their frustrations will be minimized and they will be successful.

If you *are* the company right now, prioritize and get busy on what's most important and valuable for your business to succeed. Get good at contracting out those tasks that are not the best use of your talents, skills, abilities, and passions. As Michael Gerber says in his bestselling book, *The E-Myth Revisited*, "Work *on* the business, not *in* the business."

"Work on the business, not in the business."

Shown on the next page is the continuation of the development of the TLC objective for creating this book, along with the cascading strategies and tactics to accomplish it. You can continue creating more detail using the mindmap that I revealed in the previous chapter or begin getting more detailed using a spreadsheet-type format as follows in Figure 11 on the next page.

Figure 11: Cascading a Goal into Objectives, Strategies, and Tactics

Goal 3 – Product Development: Offer products that are in high demand by our target audience.

Action Team Leader(s): Ray Madaghiele

Objectives	Strategies	Tactics
Objective A: Publish *Energize Your Business*	Strategy 1: Outline book	Tactic 1: Identify elements
		Tactic 2: Define chapters
		Tactic 3: Sequence chapters
	Strategy 2: Write manuscript	Tactic 1: Write 10 pages per day
		Tactic 2: Research best practices
		Tactic 3: Interview successful business owners
	Strategy 3: Create graphics	Tactic 1: Sketch draft graphics
		Tactic 2: Hire graphic artist
		Tactic 3: Finalize graphics
	Strategy 4: Design cover	Tactic 1: Hire graphic artist
		Tactic 2: Identify concept
		Tactic 3: Create draft cover options
		Tactic 4: Finalize cover
	Strategy 5: Publish eBook	Tactic 1: Contract with eBook publisher
		Tactic 2: Identify formatting criteria for different eBook reader platforms
		Tactic 3: Format manuscript & launch on different eBook reader platforms
	Strategy 6: Publish print book	Tactic 1: Contract with publisher
		Tactic 2: Identify formatting criteria
		Tactic 3: Upload manuscript
		Tactic 4: Upload cover & graphics
		Tactic 5: Create proof
		Tactic 6: Approve proof
		Tactic 7: Finalize book
		Tactic 8: Launch book
	Strategy 7: Marketing & Sales	Tactic 1: Get professional help
		Tactic 2: Create book website and blog
		Tactic 3: Promote on social media
		Tactic 4: Virtual book tour
		Tactic 5: Secure radio interviews
		Tactic 6: Secure TV interviews
		Tactic 7: Sales to past clients
		Tactic 8: Attract new clients

A spreadsheet is a great way to flesh out the other details that go into a comprehensive Action Plan. See the Action Plan Submittal Worksheet in Appendix C for a helpful template. Here are some considerations for developing your own Action Plans:

1. Prioritize each Goal, Objective, and Strategy

2. Ask yourself, "For each Strategy, what Tactics or tasks need to happen in order to get this done?" These are the specific day-to-day actions that need to be taken. This is also a good opportunity to get input from those who will be assigned the tasks.

3. Determine the priority (A, B, or C) for each task. An "A" priority denotes a task that definitely has to be done in order to accomplish the goal. A "B" priority task would enhance the

goal, but if it's not completed, the goal can still be achieved. A "C" priority is nice to do if you get around to it, or it can be achieved in the process of accomplishing something else. Nonetheless, it will have little effect on achieving the goal.

4. When should this task be scheduled to begin? When should it be completed?

5. How much will this task cost to complete?

6. Who will be responsible for completing this task?

7. What other resources will be needed for completing this task?

When all these steps and questions have been answered for each task, you will have the full picture of what it will take to accomplish each goal.

In addition to its guidance, this detail work will become a vital part of your financial plan and budgeting process. You'll be able to see the cash flow requirements clearly, and it will also help you to decide whether the goals need to be phased into your current operations or to be deferred to a later date.

For details on how to facilitate the Action Planning process, see the **Step-by-Step Facilitator's Guide** in the last section of this book, and the sample spreadsheet in Appendix C.

Energizing Thoughts to Ponder
for Chapter 9

1. Who should be on your Strategic Plan Steering Committee to guide the action planning process?

2. Who are the best people to assign to Action Planning Teams for each goal focus area you identified in the previous chapter? Keep the size of each team to a maximum of ten people, or else it can become unwieldy and unproductive.

3. When do you want the Action Planning Teams to complete their assigned Action Plans?

4. How do you want the Action Planning Teams to communicate their progress?

Chapter 10

Keep the Energy Flowing

"All natural laws and all of nature's plans are based upon harmonious, cooperative effort."

~Napoleon Hill
Author, *Law of Success*

In the late 1990's, when I was instructing and consulting for a corporate training company, I learned a vital lesson about the value of time and energy from a friend, entrepreneur, and colleague named Reg Couch, who was 69 years young when we met for the first time. One day, I was sitting in a staff meeting when Reg burst into the room, determined to read to the group an inspirational poem he had written. There he stood, with neatly coiffed white hair and a beard. Poised and confident, hands shaking from a neuro-muscular condition, he read to us, from his heart, with passion and enthusiasm. Even at his ripe age of wisdom, he was bubbling over with life and vitality. Then he exited as quickly as he had entered.

I said to myself, "I need to meet this guy!" so I called him to schedule lunch together.

A few days later, sitting opposite one another at a restaurant, I asked Reg how he was doing. Without hesitation, he said, "Better! Better today than yesterday, and not as good as tomorrow."

Then, he told me he was starting a new business and also operating a foundation that sponsored young, budding international musicians—a venture that was fueling his passion for classical music. As we talked, Reg purposefully took off his watch and handed it to me. Then he asked, "What time is it?" Perplexed, I stared at his watch, noticing immediately that it had no hands or numbers on its dial—just a single, bold word in capital letters: "**NOW!**"

After Reg observed my reaction—that I seemed to understand its meaning—he said, "That's right—the time is *now*. It's the most precious thing we have. Now is the most important time there is, and I am spending it the best way I know—with you." My heart melted, and we formed a close friendship.

In that moment, I realized completely that this impressive man was living each moment of his life to the fullest, always seeing, grasping, and flowing with new possibilities that aligned with his passions.

"Now is the most important time there is!"

Time is your most precious resource, and the strategic planning process is the best investment of time I know for developing an effective plan that focuses energy (time and resources) so that you and your employees are doing what is most important to achieve success and fulfillment while also being on the lookout for what else may be unfolding, poised and ready to shift direction, if warranted.

So, who is responsible for the success of your new strategic plan? Everyone!

Once your action plans are complete, the task at hand is to keep them alive, employing everyone's cooperation and collaboration. Don't let your planning book gather dust on a shelf, never to be seen again until next year's planning retreat. Allow your strategic plan to be a living, breathing guide to individual and organizational success. Done right, the strategic plan should guide everyone's actions by constantly reminding them of the most important use of their time.

Instead of feeling the burden of thinking you have to do it alone, ignite the enthusiasm and passion in your employees by involving them in making the new strategic plan come alive.

The more you involve people in its implementation, the greater will be their enthusiastic buy-in and support for the plan.

Furthermore, ask your managers to create an individual development plan for everyone in the organization such that every employee has at least one goal to actively work toward achieving. Let everyone have a piece of the puzzle so they can feel a sense of pride and ownership in the success of the organization's new direction. Allow them to feel a sense of meaning and belonging to something bigger than themselves.

Here are seven ways to engage your employees in the implementation phase:

1. **Gain their initial enthusiastic support and buy-in –** Communicate to everyone in the organization the benefits of implementing the plan and the importance of their wholehearted participation in its success. "Connect the dots" for them so they see that your actions are based upon *their* input.

2. **Involve ALL employees in the process, from the CEO to the frontline –** Give everyone the opportunity to share ideas, knowing that all ideas will be considered. This is a skillful way to tap into the vast knowledge and experience that is frequently underutilized in organizations. Allow this collaborative process to be like an artist molding a clay sculpture of the desired future state of your organization.

3. **Create Declarations of Understanding (DOUs)** – List the behaviors that will constitute a sense of support and co-operation among employees—the ways in which they can count on each other. Clarify in writing your desires and expectations regarding your direct reports, and let them reciprocate by sharing their desires and expectations with respect to you. Then, encourage your direct reports to do the same with *their* direct reports, thus creating a cascading effect throughout the organization. The DOUs help to clarify decision-making authority, solidify boundaries, and minimize unpleasant or awkward "surprises" at employee performance review time.

4. **Keep the plan alive by establishing a team of "Eagles"** – A proficient way to keep people engaged is to establish an Eagle Team (or Steering Committee) whose sole purpose is to keep the high watch and continually infuse energy into implementing the plan. This team keeps track of progress and adjusts the plan when new, unforeseen developments arise, recommending mid-course corrections to executive leadership. The team should include people from every level of the organization. Consider periodically alternating who leads the team in order to keep things fresh and exciting and build leadership skills. When building your Eagle Team, assign high-performing employees ("Eagles") from different levels and functional areas of your organization—and be sure to inform each team member that this special assignment is an honor and privilege. Remember to listen to what those on your team suggest, and act on as many ideas as possible. Failure to follow through could jeopardize the entire collaborative process.

5. **Practice transparency** – Communicate progress often with all of your employees; keep them abreast of all progress toward accomplishing the organization's vision, strategies, and goals. Be candid in your

communications. Seek input for improvements from employees at every level within the company, and listen intently to the feedback you receive. Your people will appreciate your candor and openness, and the result will be a culture built upon trust.

6. **Provide consistent and frequent communication** – Create a systematic communication plan for sharing progress, reporting on milestones achieved, and expressing appreciation for the efforts of all your team members. Make sure that stakeholders are informed at the level most appropriate for each of them. After all the energy you will have invested in listening to your employees, the last thing you want them to say is, "Why did I bother? They didn't do anything with my ideas anyway!" With regard to the absence of communication, there is a scientific principle that says, "Nature abhors a vacuum." Remember, if you and your leaders fail to keep the whole company fully informed, some employees will fill that 'vacuum' by consulting the rumor mill. And, as you have already realized, the rumor mill is quite efficient but is seldom accurate and constructive.

7. **Celebrate successes often** – To keep the fires of company enthusiasm stoked, show appreciation for all the valiant efforts of your team. This extremely effective motivator costs nothing and has a lasting, positive effect. Create a culture of acknowledgment. Show appreciation for individual and team achievements. Praise the slightest improvement. Praise every improvement. And by all means, share the wealth through bonuses and/or other concierge benefits.

Celebrate milestones. Celebrate each other. Think of fun ways to show appreciation. Give the Eagle Team free rein to keep the ideas fresh and exciting—to exercise the "creative" muscles of every one of them.

Successful companies celebrate often and use their celebrations as opportunities to reinforce their cultural values.

There is great power in appreciation. When it comes to our finances, we want our bottom-line and our investments to *appreciate*—to increase in value... to rise... to escalate. When it comes to human nature, appreciation has a similar relevance. As human beings, we all want to feel uplifted and valued—as friend, family member, employee. Remember from the previous chapter, "The deepest principle in human nature is the craving to be appreciated."

> *"The deepest principle in human nature is the craving to be appreciated."*

To illustrate the power of this principle, let me share my recent experience as an interviewer on a job interview panel. One of the applicants shared that the main reason she wanted to leave her existing job was, *she didn't feel appreciated by her boss.* When she talked with her boss about important matters, she reported, he didn't seem interested. She also observed that he was often critical. "The only thing that seems to matter to him," she said, "is the bottom-line." His lack of appreciation at the personal level had caused this valuable employee to seek employment elsewhere. Could this be happening in your organization?

Why does something as simple as showing appreciation have such a phenomenally positive effect? Because it invokes a fundamental, universal principle. Social psychologists call it the natural Law of Reciprocity. Reciprocity refers to the human tendency to respond to a positive action with an equally positive action, rewarding kind actions with kindness. Reciprocity means that, in response to friendly actions, people are frequently much nicer and much more co-operative.

Physicists call it the Law of Cause and Effect: *For every action, there is a reaction.*

Meta-physicians call it the Law of Attraction: *Like attracts like.*

Dr. Masaru Emoto, researcher and author of *Hidden Messages in Water*, who studied the effect of words on our water-dominant human physiology said, "Water has a message for the world: The world is linked together by love and gratitude . . . The words 'gratitude' and 'love' form the fundamental principles of the laws of nature and the phenomenon of life."

When we express gratitude or appreciation to another person, they feel better; and, simultaneously, we feel better at a deep, cellular level. It actually strengthens our molecular bond with each other.

Try this simple self-assessment: Do you receive far more appreciation than you deserve—yes or no? Do you regularly dish out healthy portions of honest, sincere appreciation to associates, friends, and family members—yes or no? Could there be a correlation?

The bottom-line: if you want more appreciation, show more appreciation.

If you want to brighten a person's day and lift productivity, give an honest, sincere compliment.

If you want to increase the productivity of your team, create a culture of appreciation and acknowledgment in which people are catching other people in the act of doing things right. Similar to throwing a pebble into a pond, you will send a powerful ripple of gratitude throughout your organization.

Lao Tzu said, "Your behavior influences others through a ripple effect. A ripple effect works because everyone influences everyone else. Powerful people are powerful influences."

For details on how to facilitate the Implementation Process, see the **Step-by-Step Facilitator's Guide** in the last section of the book.

Energizing Thoughts to Ponder for Chapter 10

1. What goals do you want to assign to your direct reports?

2. What are your desires and expectations regarding your direct reports?

3. What do you think your direct reports desire and expect from you?

4. Who would be a good Eagle Team member? (Hint: These are your cheerleaders, culture advocates, and party people.)

5. What are some good ways to show appreciation that will cost you or your organization little to nothing?

6. Who are the stakeholders with whom you need to communicate about the Strategic Plan?

Chapter 11

Deliver 24k Gold Service™

*"As we look ahead into the next century, leaders will
be those who empower others."*

~Bill Gates
Co-founder, Microsoft

Figure 12:
Providing 24k Gold Service™—The Gold Standard™

Do you want to improve customer loyalty and profitability
dramatically? Distinguish your organization from the competition
by encouraging your employees to live up to **The G.O.L.D.
Standard**™ by practicing the following four tenets:

<u>G</u>olden Rule – Each employee treats customers (internal and
external) like pure gold.

<u>O</u>wnership – Each employee makes decisions as though he
or she owns the company.

Love Serving All – Everyone loves his or her job and serving *all* customers.

Diamond Rule – By choosing to "walk a mile in the other person's moccasins"—truly understanding the needs and desires of their customers—your employees will discover "acres of diamonds" ready for harvesting.

Master these four simple tenets, and you will differentiate your organization from the masses by showing that you truly care about your customers by providing 24k Gold Service. Let's dig deeper into the inherent power in each of these tenets.

Golden Rule – The #1 Rule for Attracting and Retaining Customers

Here are some examples of successful organizations that deliver exemplary service by putting into practice a simple, timeless, and powerful core value—The Golden Rule. If you think it's "too touchy-feely" for your organization, think again.

How about Hewlett Packard's "The HP Way"— which focuses on respect and concern for the individual. It is simply the Golden Rule, which says, "Do unto others as you would have them do unto you."

HP was identified in *Built to Last*, by James Collins and Jerry Porras, as one of the most successful visionary companies of the past hundred years.

"Do unto others as you would have them do unto you."

One of the most popular business books of all time, Dale Carnegie's *How to Win Friends and Influence People*, dedicates over half its contents to illustrating different facets of "The Golden Rule." Since the book's release in 1936, it has sold more than 15 million copies. Today, it is still listed on bestseller lists along with other current top-selling business books.

Not convinced yet? One of the oldest and largest business associations, Rotary International, advocates applying "The 4-Way Test" in making sound business decisions.

Before deciding a course of action, apply "The 4-Way Test" to the things we think, say and do:

1. Is it the truth?

2. Is it fair to all concerned?

3. Will it build goodwill and better friendships?

4. Will it be beneficial to all concerned?

These are all facets of "The Golden Rule!"

Conclusion: It simply makes good business sense to invoke this universal principle of service in order to attract and retain customers (and valued employees).

Whenever I facilitate the core values portion of the strategic planning process, I begin by asking the participants to brainstorm these two types of Golden Rule questions:

*   *"How do you like to be treated as an employee?"* and

*   *"How do your customers like to be treated?"*

Answering these simple, yet profound, questions will establish or clarify the behavioral values of your organization. As we discussed previously, the greater the number of employees you involve in defining "their own behavioral values," the greater will be their enthusiastic buy-in for implementing them.

You will find that these values also provide a worthwhile tool for measuring individual and team service success.

So, how do *you* like to be treated?

Ownership – Create a Service Culture of O.W.N.E.R.S.H.I.P.

What would it be like to work in an organization in which employees are encouraged to make decisions as though they own the company? Here's what's possible...

Nordstrom understands the power of ownership as it relates to providing exemplary service. Here's their half-page employee handbook in its entirety:

Welcome to Nordstrom. We're glad to have you with our Company. Our number one goal is to provide outstanding customer service. Set both your personal and professional goals high. We have great confidence in your ability to achieve them. So our employee handbook is very simple. We have only one rule...

Our only rule: Use good judgment in all situations.

Please feel free to ask your department manager, store manager or personnel manager any question at any time.

How's that for, in a nutshell, instilling ownership?

"Our only rule: Use good judgment in all situations."

How well are you and your organization practicing this level of ownership? Try these **OWNERSHIP Principles** on for size:

Optimism – Owners maintain a positive, "can do" attitude, always "looking up" for opportunities and possibilities, even in the midst of chaos. They understand that we create our tomorrows through our thoughts, words and actions today.

We Attitude – Owners are team players who understand the power of synergy and make decisions that are in the best interest of the whole. They give credit where credit is due.

iNnovative – Owners fearlessly express their creativity without worrying whether they will fail or look bad, understanding that each failure is a steppingstone to success. They are always looking for ways to improve processes, systems, and performance.

Elevate – Owners are never satisfied with the status quo. They continuously raise their own bar to higher levels of personal effectiveness and productivity—and inspire others to do the same.

Responsibility – Owners are accountable and assume 100% responsibility for their thoughts, words, and actions. They see themselves as active contributors to the organization's success—and their own.

Solution-Focused – Owners do not dwell on problems but instead focus their attention on solutions—converting problems into goals. They do not waste energy on blaming and finger-pointing.

Helpful – Owners enjoy "Wowing" their customers—internally and externally. They seize each interaction as a 'moment of truth' for taking the initiative to serve before being asked.

Integrity – Owners do what they say they will do and follow through on their commitments. They model the organization's values and operate consistently with policies and procedures.

Productivity – Owners know how to manage their own enthusiasm and energy. They prioritize their goals so that everything they do is highly focused and productive.

Imagine what your life and your organization could be like with such a culture of ownership. The words "fulfilling" and "successful" come to mind.

What is your organization doing to create a service culture of ownership?

Love Serving All – What's Love Got to Do with Business?

What if this is true: "It's all about love"?

"What's love got to do with business?" you ask. In a nutshell, everything!

- Customers and employees who feel loved are more loyal to your company.
- Employees who love their bosses and their jobs perform better.
- Customers and employees who feel loved share their experiences with others.

Simply put: Love aspires. Love inspires. Love grows.

"Simply put: Love aspires. Love inspires. Love grows."

Let's look at two extraordinary companies, both of which were launched in 1971—more than 45 years ago—operating with love as an essential core value.

Have you ever enjoyed a burger and a beer at a Hard Rock Café? Did you know that the company was founded by two hippies who chose love, peace, and rock-'n-roll as their mantra? Isaac Tigrett and Peter Morton were two shaggy-haired Americans who just wanted to find a good American burger while living in London. They built their first café on London's Hyde Park corner as the first "classless" restaurant in the class-laden English society.

Today there are more than 175 Hard Rock locations, which include restaurants, hotels, casinos, and live music venues in 55 countries. Emblazoned on the wall of every property is, "Love All, Serve All." It is the life—and business—success principle that Tigrett borrowed from his guru in India.

The Seminole Tribe acquired the Hard Rock companies in 2007, continuing to keep its love-based culture alive. Their mottos are still visible: "Love All, Serve All," "Take Time to Be Kind," "All Is One," and "Save the Planet." And how's this for a core value: "Deliver kick-ass service."

"Love All, Serve All"

Southwest Airlines is another company that fearlessly embraces love ("LUV") as a fundamental principle.

Since 1971, Southwest has continued to differentiate itself from other carriers with exemplary customer service delivered by nearly 45,000 employees to more than 100 million customers annually. They have been named to *Fortune's* 2014 list of World's Most Admired Companies for the 20th consecutive year; and, notably, it is the only commercial airline to rank in the Top Ten.

In their own words (from the Southwest Airlines website), here's a glimpse of how Southwest infuses their culture with "LUV"…

> **What's LUV?** *Southwest has been in LUV with our Customers from the very beginning. Therefore, it's fitting that we began service … from Love Field in Dallas … As*

our company and customers grew, our LUV grew, too! With the prettiest flight attendants serving 'Love Bites' on our planes, and determined employees issuing tickets from our 'Love Machines', we changed the face of the airline industry throughout the 1970s. Then, in 1977, our stock was listed on the New York Stock Exchange under the ticker symbol LUV. Over the ensuing years, our LUV has spread from coast to coast and border to border, thanks to our hardworking employees and their LUV for customer service…

Southwest Airlines' number one priority is to ensure the personal safety of each Southwest customer and employee. Beyond this, we follow The Golden Rule, meaning that we treat each other the way we want to be treated, which is why doing the right thing by our employees and customers is so inherent to who we are as a company. We believe in Living the Southwest Way, which is to have a "Warrior Spirit," a "Servant's Heart," and a "Fun-LUVing Attitude." Within each of these categories are specific behaviors to help us be a safe, profitable, and fun place to work.

So, who says love doesn't last? Indeed, love has everything to do with good business! Love is lasting—living in the hearts of all the people you and your organization touch.

If Hard Rock Café and Southwest Airlines can inoculate their companies with love and achieve lasting success, so can yours.

What are you and your organization doing to spread the love?

The Diamond Rule – Do this to Truly Understand Your Customers

What will it take for your company to be the "happiest place on earth?"

During this time of the year, I daydream about past family vacations at Disneyland. What makes it "the happiest place on earth"?

Several years ago, I attended a Disney seminar for leaders and was amazed at their organization's attention to their customers' needs and desires.

Disney employees exemplify what I call "The Diamond Rule: *Strive honestly to see things from the other person's point of view.*"

"The Diamond Rule: Strive honestly to see things from the other person's point of view."

If you have ever visited Disneyland, you may not be aware of how much the employees understand you, their customer, intimately:

- The employees strive to minimize distractions and expedite check-in at their hotels because they know your family's nerves are already frazzled from the long, exhausting trip to get there. They know the last thing you need is more stimulation at that moment.

- You won't find an outside newspaper for sale anywhere on their property because they know you have come there to escape from the "real world."

- Every employee knows the location of the nearest restroom because they know you have pushed your bladder to its limits and will need to make a mad dash to get there in time.

- Trash receptacles are placed no more than 30 steps apart because they know just how long you are willing to hold onto your trash before dropping it.

- Suspenseful entertainment is provided while you twist and turn your way with great anticipation in long lines that lead to each attraction. As a result, you lose track of time and don't mind the wait very much.

- Disney employees are called "Cast Members" as a way of reminding them that when they enter the property, "It's show time!"—and their most important audience is you and your family.

Disney diligently studies the needs and desires of their customers. They walk a mile in the shoes of all their customers. They practice the Diamond Rule with fervor!

How well do you understand your customers' points of view?

The surest way to reach all your goals is by building exemplary "24k Gold Service™" into your strategic plan. Instill this belief: "See every opportunity as a moment of truth to harvest the gold and diamonds that already exist in the hearts and minds of your employees and customers." As a noteworthy benefit, providing 24k Gold Service™ is fun and rewarding.

"See every opportunity as a moment of truth to harvest the gold and diamonds that already exist in the hearts and minds of your employees and customers."

For details on how to facilitate an Ownership discussion, see the **Step-by-Step Facilitator's Guide** in the last section of the book.

Energizing Thoughts to Ponder for Chapter 11

---

1. How do you like to be treated?

2. How do your customers like to be treated?

3. What is your organization doing to create a service culture of ownership?

4. What are you and your organization doing to spread the love?

5. How well do you understand your customers' (internal and external) points of view?

4th Phase: Get Results

*"A business is like an automobile,
it has to be driven,
in order to get results."*

~Bertie Charles Forbes

Financial journalist, author, and founder of *Forbes Magazine*

In this section, you will explore measuring your progress, ebbing and flowing as conditions change, and dispelling myths about strategic planning.

Chapter 12

Measure Your Progress

"My measure of success is whether I'm fulfilling my mission."
~Robert Kiyosaki
Author, *Rich Dad, Poor Dad*

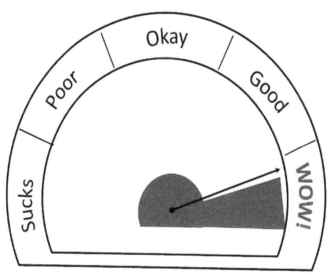

Figure 13: The WOW Meter

How are you going to know how well you're doing in achieving your mission, vision, and goals?

It's time to establish performance targets that everyone will be working toward during the next two to three years. Every goal-objective-strategy should be measured in some manner. That means establishing measurement factors: some organizations call them Critical Success Factors (CSFs); others call them Key Performance Indicators (KPIs); still others call them Critical Success Indicators (CSIs). It is not important what you choose to call them. What is important is that you develop some sort of measurements to know whether or not you are always on track to achieve the results you desire.

Begin by thinking about the important metrics that indicate success. What are they for your organization? Most likely there will be some differences for each business area or line of business (LOB). Here are some possibilities:

- Gross sales
- Profitability
- Employee retention (of valuable employees)
- Employee turnover
- Defects/returns
- Production time
- Production rate
- On-time delivery
- Inventory turnover
- Sales growth
- Market share
- Cash reserve
- Research and development expenditures
- Marketing return-on-investment
- Overhead rate
- Number of users
- Number of members
- Customer satisfaction
- Employee satisfaction
- and so on, depending on the nature of your business.

Once you have determined the important factors for each line of business, link every goal, objective, and strategy to one or more of them. Make the targets relevant, real, and trackable. Consider creating tracking spreadsheets for each performance indicator similar to Figure 14 that shows performance targets for each line of business.

Lines of Business	Performance Targets		
	Year 1	Year 2	Year 3
1.			
2.			
3.			
TOTAL			

Figure 14: Performance Targets

First, it might be helpful to have your leaders ponder this question: "What can we be the best at in the world?"—or, at least, the best in your demographic area or industry.

Once you have identified your measurements, monitor both individual and organizational progress. Keep your employees informed by reporting progress at least monthly. For more critical goals, you may need to report weekly or even daily.

The important thing is to establish monitoring systems that can give you real-time data. The systems can be high tech or low tech, depending on your comfort level and preferences.

Years ago, I worked for a seminar company that reported daily sales numbers on huge whiteboards for each sales professional for each scheduled seminar. During our weekly meetings, we were able to see, at a glance, the big (and small) picture. It worked effectively for that organization. We also had the option to review our sales numbers in real time via computer-generated reports.

A company that has mastered the science of measurement is Able Engineering. Since 1982, Able has helped aircraft operators and fleet owners safely reduce operating costs by providing resourceful solutions. They expanded their business in the 1990s to include FAA-approved parts, along with repairs, overhauls, exchanges, and partnerships.

More than 30 years after opening their doors, they continue to extend their capabilities and grow their team. While many things have changed over the decades, one thing has remained the same: Able's unrelenting focus on being the best value alternative around for aircraft parts and maintenance.

Every employee at Able is assigned to at least one team that regularly meets to discuss progress and resolve issues, using what they call computer "dashboards" that show the status of everything they are measuring. This type of system can be especially valuable if you have a production or sales environment.

Lee Benson, founder and CEO of Able Engineering, has developed a real-time measurement system in which all employees can update their progress on assigned strategies every day.

The leadership at Able encourages each person to behave like a top-performing employee. Able has created a culture of focused intention in which everyone is helping to cascade the strategies throughout every level of the organization. Every person and team is measured by how well they are accomplishing their assigned strategies. Everything Able does is measured and optimized to achieve results, including the effectiveness of living their core values.

Once you have established measurements for your lines of business, it's time to link them back to each employee.

As discussed in Chapter 10, every employee should have an individual development plan. I suggest that for your weekly one-on-one meetings you build in an agenda item to review the progress your employees are making with their assigned goals (if not weekly, at least monthly). No one likes surprises during an annual employee performance review. Keep everyone informed, and manage desires and expectations to assure that they remain reasonable and attainable.

Use your measurement systems as a trigger for celebrating milestones achieved for individuals, teams, and the company as a whole. Celebrate often! Nothing energizes employees more than their being acknowledged and feeling appreciated.

You don't have to be too sophisticated. Choose a system that you will continue to use. The important thing is to know at any given time where you stand with respect to making progress toward your goals.

For details on how to facilitate the implementing, measuring, and refining phase, see the **Step-by-Step Facilitator's Guide** in the last section of the book.

Energizing Thoughts to Ponder for Chapter 12

1. What are important areas to measure that will indicate your company's success?

2. What measurement systems do you already have in place?

3. What measurement systems do you need to establish in order to monitor individual and organizational success?

Chapter 13

Ebb and Flow with Conditions

"Whatever is flexible and flowing will tend to grow.
Whatever is rigid and blocked will atrophy and die."

~Lao Tzu
from the *Tao Te Ching*

Gentle flowing mountain stream

The only constant in the universe is change. Everything is ebbing and flowing—all the time. The economy is ebbing and flowing. Your industry standards are ebbing and flowing. Customer expectations are ebbing and flowing. Your employees' lives, needs, and desires are ebbing and flowing.

Therefore, a strategic plan should be flexible, not rigid. Consider it to be like a piece of clay that you continue to mold because of new conditions and input. Circumstances and markets are always changing, and so should your plan. Help your employees to understand why changes are important, and then engage them in being important parts of implementing the changes your company needs to make. This will foster a spirit of ownership.

> *"A strategic plan should be flexible, not rigid.*
> *Consider it to be like a piece of clay that you continue*
> *to mold because of new conditions and input."*

Changes will always affect your teams. Whether it is a change in the scope of their responsibilities or a change in team members, train your team leaders so they understand team dynamics and how to keep people engaged. Provide your leaders with tools for facilitating groups, group problem solving, mediation, and team building.

The following example may help you to understand more fully the natural cycle of team development, especially as it relates to change.

Recently, I enjoyed working with a passionate and diverse team of community leaders. Some were veterans of the four-year-old committee. Others had been members of the group for a very short time—in fact, one had joined that day. They came from different ethnic and cultural backgrounds, they were at different formal education levels and worldly experience, and they had different opinions about how to do things. But they shared the same passion and desire to make a meaningful difference in their community.

The team had been experiencing conflicts, including communication issues that were getting in the way of making progress on significant goals. Sound familiar?

They brought me in to facilitate their annual retreat and guide them to create alignment, reach agreements, and set priorities for the following year. I began by sharing what I call the "Cycle of

Teams." See Figure 15. It helped them put things into perspective and understand that what they had been experiencing as a team was natural. I shared that every team progresses through these four phases—usually multiple times:

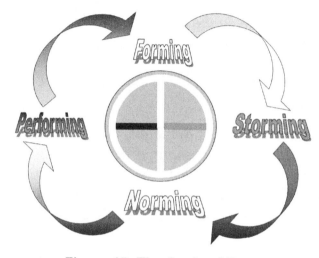

Figure 15: The Cycle of Teams

1. **Forming** – *The team is formed. People come together and begin checking each other out and discovering why each person is there. Everyone is pleasant. No one wants to rock the boat. Everyone is becoming clearer about his or her various tasks, roles and responsibilities, and how those elements fit into the big picture. It is analogous to dipping a toe into a body of water to test the temperature before fully committing to dive in. This phase is vital in order to reach the next level of maturity in the cycle…*

2. **Storming** – *In this phase, people are refining their understanding of their roles and responsibilities and are becoming bolder and more comfortable about sharing their thoughts and feelings. People are more authentic in expressing their unique personalities. Conflicts naturally arise as team members share differing ideas*

and opinions. They are prone to take a stand on key issues. This phase is vital to reach the next level of maturity in the cycle…

3. **Norming** – *Conflicts are resolved. The group becomes clear about its collective vision, mission, and goals. Team members understand their individual roles and responsibilities. The group reaches agreement regarding what is in the best interest of all concerned. Individuals detach from their selfish positions and align with what's important to the group as a whole. This phase is essential in reaching the next level of maturity in the cycle…*

4. **Performing** – *Things are humming along. Actions are being implemented. The group synergistically moves forward in alignment with its vision, mission, and goals, with an eye on doing what's in the best interest of all concerned. Communication is compassionate, open and free-flowing. Everything is progressing according to plan. People feel great about what they are accomplishing together as a team.*

Note: Teams don't go through the four phases of the cycle only once. It's continual! Whenever a new team member joins, or an existing member leaves, or the team goals change, the team leader needs to guide the team through the cycle again. The good news is that it typically takes much less energy to complete the process than it does during the initial cycle.

After we completed the annual retreat, the team members had a greater understanding and appreciation of each other as well as a unified understanding of their direction together. They could see where they were with regard to the "Cycle of Teams" and understand what it was going to take to reach the next phase.

It is also important to accept that people may have different responses to stressors that are triggered by change. Some people perceive change as exciting and invigorating. Others view it with fear and panic. Still others remain indifferent—almost numb—clinging to a wait-and-see attitude. It is all a matter of individual perspective and perception.

> *"It is also important to accept that people may have different responses to stressors that are triggered by change."*

Your job as a leader is to communicate clearly the benefits (the *why*) of any changes being considered.

An even better strategy is to involve your Eagle Team in researching possible changes and then have them communicate their findings to the rest of your employees, their peers.

Since everything in the universe is continuously evolving and transforming to its next energy state, why would it be any different for your organization?

For details on how to facilitate change when conditions are ebbing and flowing, see the **Step-by-Step Facilitator's Guide** in the last section of the book.

Energizing Thoughts to Ponder for Chapter 13

1. Are there any changes you foresee on the horizon?

2. How could these changes affect your company?

3. How will you communicate these changes to your employees?

4. How can you engage your employees in dealing with the changes?

Chapter 14

Dispel the Myths

Myth – *False belief: a widely held but mistaken belief*

~Encarta Dictionary

Strategic Planning should be engaging and inspiring

Now that you have reached this point in our work together, my hope is that you have a clearer picture of the merits of completing a strategic plan for your own company.

At the beginning, I identified several myths that sometimes surface during discussions about strategic planning. Hopefully, after having read the selection of inspiring stories and principles described so far, you now have a better understanding of the truth that you can create a strategic road map to success for your business.

So now let's play Myth Buster.

Myth #1: Small business owners don't need a strategic plan unless they intend to get money from investors or banks.

Myth Buster #1: Even if you are starting a business with your own funds (similar to Greentoes, which had a powerful purpose that propelled them forward), your strategic plan will help you create a clear set of blueprints in order to manifest your inspired concept.

Myth #2: Strategic planning is boring drudgery to be tolerated, much like swallowing awful-tasting medicine that's good for you in the long run.

Myth Buster #2: Strategic planning is, in fact, a fun way to make your unique brand come alive (similar to what Johnny Cupcakes has done so masterfully). Every strategy and action Johnny Cupcakes takes is an opportunity for him to play the trickster and have fun with his employees and customers. You, too, can make your planning and implementation fun.

Myth #3: The strategic planning process is a hard, complex, heady process that only someone with an MBA could possibly appreciate and understand.

Myth Buster #3: Strategic planning can tap into the unique wisdom and understanding of your employees. You don't have to use complicated terms and models. Instead, keep it simple and understandable by all (much like the Leech Lake Band of Ojibwe did by using the Tree of Success to accent their cultural beliefs about nature, balance and organization).

Myth #4: Strategic planning is an esoteric process, reserved for leaders in Fortune 500 companies and created on corporate 'mountain-tops'. Then, management delivers the completed tablets to its loyal subjects in the form of new laws to follow.

Myth Buster #4: You can use strategic planning as a way to strengthen collaboration and cooperation, (much like Arizona Cooperative Therapies (ACT) used the process to reenergize and engage their members and create alignment around a loftier mission and a concrete action plan).

Myth #5: Employees have more important things to do than to waste time planning. Besides, frontline employees don't care about planning and have very little to contribute to the process anyway.

Myth Buster #5: Everyone wants to be part of something great, and each person wants to be heard. The Salt River Pima-Maricopa Indian Community continues to experience powerful results by giving every employee and Community Member a voice. The Community's collective vision has proven to be very lucrative for its members. Your employees do, indeed, care—and have a lot to offer.

Myth #6: Strategic plans are just nice pronouncements that collect dust on a bookshelf, to be opened again only at next year's company retreat.

Myth Buster #6: Even if the type of planning process you are accustomed to has been a yearly exercise in futility, you can change all that and make the process more meaningful. Do something similar to Sitewire's dynamic strategic roadmaps process every two months, which helps them re-focus their resources on what matters most and keeps their enduring cultural values alive.

If you haven't yet begun your organization's strategic planning process, what are you waiting for? Now's your time to shine!

Go ahead . . . get clear, get organized, get going, and get results!

The following section is a **<u>Step-by-Step Facilitator's Guide</u>** that reveals my proven facilitation secrets, tools and tips that can make your process be engaging and inspiring for all involved.

Step-by-Step Facilitator's Guide

Fa•cil•i•tate – *Simplify process; to make (something) easier; to help cause (something); to help (something) run more smoothly and effectively*

~Merriam Webster Dictionary

Introduction

Facilitation is both an art and a science.

Throughout this section you will be guided to determine the best way to proceed with your own custom-designed strategic planning process for your organization.

I will reveal my personal secrets, tools, and tips so you can create each element of the process such that it will engage and energize your employees on your journey to get clear, get organized, get going, and get results!

Let's begin by designing your unique process.

First, we will look at how you can *Set the Right Energy,* including how to . . .

- Choose the right facilitator

- Design the right process

- Send the right message

- Create the right environment

Then, you will learn my steps for *Facilitating the Strategic Planning Elements.*

As you're planning to plan and reading the detailed steps that follow, keep in mind the following sequence of steps to perform before you launch into your strategic planning process:

1. Be sure that the leaders of the company are clear in their own minds that they want to engage their employees in a strategic planning process.

2. Bring the owners and top executives together in a meeting to agree and commit to going through the strategic planning process. Then decide whether an outside facilitator or an internal neutral facilitator will guide the process.

3. Decide what format will work best for your organization and who will attend each session.

4. Enlist the executive team to invite the participants to join the process.

5. Craft a communication to send to all employees in the organization that gives an overview of the process and shares how they will be involved. Give everyone the opportunity to provide input and feedback as the process unfolds.

Chapter 15

Set the Right Energy

"Enjoyment is an incredible energizer to the human spirit."

~John C. Maxwell
Author, *The 5 Levels of Leadership*

Creating an energizing and fun experience

Setting the right energy upfront will ensure that the strategic planning process flows smoothly and that people will participate whole-heartedly with the right attitude.

Within this chapter you will discover how to:
- choose the right facilitator;
- design the right process;
- send the right message; and
- create the right atmosphere.

1) Choose the Right Facilitator

Fa•cil•i•ta•tor — *One that facilitates; especially: one that helps to bring about an outcome (as learning, productivity, or communication) by providing indirect or unobtrusive assistance, guidance, or supervision*

~Merriam Webster Dictionary

The success of your strategic planning process depends upon selecting the right facilitator. This person will be the foundation upon which everything is built during the process.

It is critical that you choose a neutral facilitator(s) in order to guarantee that everyone's voice will be heard. An experienced facilitator will guide the process without bias, ask the tough questions, and ensure that everyone has an opportunity to provide input. A skilled, seasoned facilitator will keep things fun, engaging, and on track by using an array of tools in his or her facilitation tool box—including storyboarding, small group activities, teambuilding elements, interactive dialogue, and intimate experiences—all seamlessly interwoven throughout the natural unfoldment of the process.

The *science* of facilitation is the step-by-step activity. It is *what* needs to be done to complete each element of the process, while progressively asking the right questions at the right time—each question building upon the next.

The *art* of facilitation is *how* you go about accomplishing it. It involves sensing the energy of the participants and knowing when to ask a tough question that will reveal the "elephant in the room"—a vital issue that is screaming for attention and crying out to be resolved. The *art* requires listening beneath the words for deeper meaning. It entails using uplifting energy and wit to lighten up tense situations.

The success of your strategic planning process will depend upon how safe people feel in sharing their deepest thoughts and feelings. For this level of comfort to occur, participants need to believe that the facilitator is a neutral party without a political or predetermined agenda. When done with pure intent, being a facilitator is a selfless role.

"The success of your strategic planning process will depend upon how safe people feel in sharing their deepest thoughts and feelings."

If, as a leader in your organization, you are thinking of facilitating the process yourself, here are three crucial questions to ask yourself: (1) "Can I be truly objective?", (2) "Will my employees be open and honest with me as their facilitator and share what's on their minds?", and (3) "Do I really have the time to dedicate to facilitating the process?" If your answer is 'no' to either question, you may want to consider hiring an outside facilitator or appointing a neutral facilitator who can answer 'yes' to all these questions.

Whatever your choice, select a facilitator who will courageously ask the tough questions and involve everyone in the process.

Select a Facilitator Who is Skilled at "Herding Cats"

Yes, sometimes facilitating groups feels like herding cats. Why? Because the more diverse the viewpoints and personalities of the participants, the greater are the chances that chaos will unfold during the process. However, despite the resulting discomfort, these times of natural turmoil are also the greatest opportunities for transformation.

Don't get me wrong. I love facilitating groups, and I love (most) cats. However, sometimes, facilitating in the midst of the chaos, I find it difficult to see how we're going to accomplish what we set out to do given all the group dynamics in play. Have you ever run into this problem?

Even Wikipedia acknowledges this phenomenon as follows:

Herding cats *may denote: An idiomatic saying that refers to an attempt to control or organize a class of entities which are uncontrollable or chaotic. Implies a task that is extremely difficult or impossible to do, primarily due to chaotic factors.*

The chaos that can ensue—and, as a result, inhibit group progress—may be caused by factors such as differences in culture, age, language, sex, education, personal agendas, and a host of other elements. Interestingly enough, though, the richness of this diversity produces the very dynamics that make the process of facilitating groups especially interesting, rewarding, and valuable for cultivating fresh, creative ideas for your organization—that is, if you are effective at "herding cats."

The key to channeling constructively all that pent-up potential energy of diverse groups is to equip yourself with the right tools, prepared to deal with whatever arises.

"The key to channeling constructively all that pent-up potential energy of diverse groups is to equip yourself with the right tools, prepared to deal with whatever arises."

Here are some of my favorite group facilitation tools and tips for captivating the attention of participants and accomplishing meeting objectives:

1. **Clear Meeting Objectives** – Prior to the facilitation, get together with key leaders and stakeholders to define the objectives of the upcoming meeting. These objectives are your ultimate targets, or goals, to accomplish.

2. **Written Agenda** – Seems obvious, doesn't it? You'd be surprised at how many meetings I have attended at which people don't know why they are there. A written agenda, at the very least, provides a good framework to channel discussions. Sending it out to the participants before the meeting is a bonus.

3. **Declarations of Understanding** – I begin every facilitated meeting by asking the participants, "What are your desires and expectations for this meeting and of me." I capture their ideas on a flipchart. Then I share with the participants what I desire and expect of them, listing everything on another flipchart. Next, I hang

both flipcharts on a wall so we can all refer to them throughout the meeting, if necessary, in order to keep things on track. My favorite desires and expectations of participants are:

- Respect each other's opinions
- Participate wholeheartedly
- Hold honest, candid discussions
- Share air time
- Honor confidentiality
- Keep discussions focused on the topic
- Be on time, and
- Have fun!

4. **Involvement** – Make the meeting fun, engaging and interesting by constantly changing the dynamics. Use open-ended questions to get participants talking—their air time should be about ten times more than the amount of your air time. If you, as the facilitator, talk too much, you will never fully realize the value of the participants' contributions. Also, be sure to get people up from their chairs and moving about from time to time. One way is to let them get up to vote (with smiley-face or star stickers) on the group ideas that have already been captured on flipcharts. This is the "physical exercise" part of your program.

5. **Spare the Slides** – Too many wordy slides are boring and put people to sleep. Use words sparingly on your slides—just enough to tee up an agenda item, exercise, or story. And, remember the famous saying, "A picture is worth a thousand words."

6. **Storyboarding** – I love to use colorful Post-It Notes as an active, enjoyable way to gather participant input, using their own words. It is also an effective way to diffuse dominant personalities and give everyone (even the quietest, contemplative ones) equal opportunity to

provide input during the process. It's a great way to keep people focused on the agenda item being discussed, and it moves things along much more quickly.

7. **Bin Items** – During storyboarding time, if the group starts to get off track by discussing something other than what is on the agenda, capture the item/idea on a flipchart labeled "Bin" so it can be addressed at another time. This action has a very valuable two-fold effect: (1) It lets participants know that you heard them and that their ideas won't be forgotten, and (2) it allows you, as the facilitator, to move on and refocus everyone's attention on that day's agenda.

8. **Small Group Activities** – Use small group activities when you need to hone in on different facets of an idea. Afterwards, bring everyone together again as a large group and allow the leaders from each small group to share their results, encouraging participants from the larger group to add their input, too. This enables you to work efficiently on several dimensions of a topic simultaneously. As an added benefit, this method has the effect of taming the herd.

9. **Strategic Breaks** – Let participants take a breather after intense discussions or when they become a little giddy. Also, if their eyes are glazing over or turning yellow, it's time for a break. Let them clear their minds and tend to their other physical needs.

10. **Acknowledgment** – Post the entire group's work on the walls during the session so participants can see what they have accomplished during their time together. Compliment them sincerely on their great work from time to time. Let them see the progress they are making toward completing the agenda items and give them encouragement that there is a light at the end of the tunnel—and it's not a train.

I hope these tips help you to enjoy facilitating groups as much as I do.

Select a Facilitator Who is a
Master at Building Trust

As a facilitator, earning the trust of the group is paramount. How else can you really build relationships but on a solid foundation of trust?

Recently a friend and long-standing client of mine asked me to help facilitate a board retreat for a diverse community group. My friend let me know that the chairperson of that group had been betrayed in the past by people who had come in to "help" the group but turned out to have had their own hidden agendas. "Trust could be an issue," my friend warned me. For the purpose of this story, I'll call the chairperson of the community group Carmella as an alias.

I knew that a phone call or email to Carmella wouldn't work and that we needed to meet face-to-face in order to experience each other's humanity. Carmella agreed to meet, and I went to that get-together with an open mind and an open heart. I knew that her trust would have to be earned in this short meeting. I also knew that I would be leaving town immediately after our meeting, not returning until the day of the board retreat. So, it was essential for me to use our time together in such a way as to melt her fears away.

Soon after exchanging introductions and polite greetings, we sat down at the table opposite each other. Carmella promptly confessed, "I don't know if I can trust you." I replied calmly, "Listen to your heart."

During the remainder of our meeting, I used the following ten notions that helped me build a solid foundation of trust with her for our upcoming work together:

1. I decided not to take anything she said personally.

2. I remained positive, continuously looking for ways to elevate the conversation to the highest level possible.

3. I was intent on getting her to reveal why she was passionate about her Community.

4. I asked thoughtful questions to understand her unique situation, issues and objectives.

5. I listened attentively, seeking to understand the whole picture and how I could best serve her, the group, and her Community.

6. I respected her position as chairperson and genuinely cared about the goals of the project and the people involved.

7. I focused on ways to help her and the group to solve their problems and reach their goals.

8. I maintained soft eye contact during our entire conversation, letting her know my sincerity.

9. I made sure to communicate my interest in a manner congruent with my words by physically leaning toward her with an open-body posture.

10. I lived my agreement with her. Not only did I email the promised draft of the agenda to her but also I sent it a day early (under-promise and over-deliver). And, as discussed, the agenda matched the objectives.

As you can imagine, this story has a happy ending. My meeting with Carmella went very well. To confirm, I asked her at the end of our meeting, "Do you feel you can trust me now?" She said, "Yes!" In the end, the Community Member retreat was a great success because Carmella and I had worked together side-by-side to accomplish *our* objectives.

My hope is that these ideas will help you (or your facilitator) to earn the trust of your strategic planning participants.

Are you still undecided about whether to use an internal or external facilitator? The list of pros and cons in Figure 16 on the next page may help.

Figure 16: Pros and cons of internal and external facilitators

Type of Facilitator	Pros	Cons
Internal	Less expensive outside investment	May not be skilled enough as a facilitator
	Familiar face	There could be internal participant biases toward the facilitator
	Knowledge of the organization's politics and culture	The outcome may be the "same old, same old," rather than a different result generated by "thinking out of the box"
	Can control the outcome	Participants may feel stifled or believe that the outcome has been pre-ordained
	Scheduling the sessions may be more flexible because you don't have to work within an external facilitator's schedule	May not have built sufficient trust to bring forth what is on people's minds and in their hearts
		Facilitator role is the primary focus, so will not be able to participate in the process
External	Effective and efficient guiding of the process, based upon years of practice/experience	Monetary outside investment
	Offers a different perspective from the outside looking in	Finding someone who is the right fit to guide the process
	Ensures that everyone participates equally	Will need to come up to speed regarding company terminology
	Skilled at working with diverse groups	Will have to learn about some company politics, personalities, and team dynamics
	Remains neutral with no biases or hidden agendas	May have to conform to facilitator's schedule
	Asks the tough questions	May "stir up the mud" or address the "sacred cows"

Hiring a Skilled External Facilitator

When hiring an external facilitator, you'll want to do your research. Ask yourself these questions:

1. Does he/she have suitable experience?

2. Will his/her style of facilitating fit with our existing culture or with the culture we want to create?

3. Will our team resonate with his/her personality?

4. Will he/she allow us time to create our own planning elements in our own words so we have enthusiastic buy-in?

5. What deliverables will we receive in exchange for our investment of time and money? (For example, when I facilitate, I include all pre-meetings, pre-work, facilitation supplies, participant guidebooks, summary reports, and a follow-up debriefing call as part of the facilitator fees. Travel expenses are additional.)

Training Your Internal Facilitator(s)

If you are planning to facilitate your own process, it is important to provide sufficient training for whoever will be playing the role of facilitator.

Also, it is imperative to select the right person with the right temperament, one who has already earned the trust of your employees. Here are some traits and strengths of an excellent facilitator: good communicator, good listener, patient, observant, problem solver, mediator, good writer, trustworthy, pleasant but candid, enthusiastic, and energetic.

Whomever you select, he/she must be willing to remain neutral and not participate by adding his/her personal input, which may skew the results.

Invest in your facilitator(s) by providing them with the following skill-building training:

- Group facilitation
- Leading effective meetings
- Communication (oral and written)
- Public speaking
- Mediation and conflict resolution
- Group problem-solving
- Teambuilding
- Project management

2) Design the Right Process

R. Buckminster Fuller said, *"People should think things out fresh and not just accept conventional terms and the conventional way of doing things."*

So it is with designing your own strategic planning process.

What is the best way to structure the process for your organization? It depends on several important factors: (1) Maximum timeframe to which participants are willing to commit; (2) People who will be involved in the different phases of the plan; and (3) Compatibility of work schedules.

Larger companies usually require more time to complete the strategic plan than do small businesses. I liken the process to the act of steering an ocean liner versus maneuvering a sailboat. An ocean liner (large company) will need more time and to swing a large arc in order to turn. A small sailboat (small business) can change direction rapidly.

The key to a successful strategic plan is to involve as many employees in the process as is practically possible in order to achieve enthusiastic buy-in and support. Keep in mind that the process of engaging employees and building teams is just as valuable as the resultant strategic plan. Therefore, you'll want to be assured that all the key participants can commit to being at all the scheduled strategic planning sessions. If they cannot be present, you will find yourself rehashing a great deal of information already covered so they come up to speed.

"The key to a successful strategic plan is to involve as many employees in the process as is practically possible in order to achieve enthusiastic buy-in and support."

Shown below is my estimate of the amount of time necessary to complete each element of the strategic planning process. The times shown will also depend upon whether you have already done some work on those elements. If you have, you can most likely reduce the amount of time. The time to complete each element will also depend upon the number of participants in the session and how well versed they are in strategic planning. You may also find it helpful to integrate some teaching segments that give examples of the elements before you begin working on them. This gets everyone on the same page, starting from the same point of reference. I have also found that because of the degree of focused mental and emotional work, six to seven hours per day is a good maximum target.

- Create Declarations of Understanding (30 minutes)

- Complete Circle of Success Assessment (1 hour)

- Clarify your organization's Core Purpose (2 hours)

- Identify your organization's Core Values (2 hours)

- Create your organization's Mission statement (2 hours)—provided you have already identified your Purpose and Values

- Capture your Leadership Team's Vision (4 hours)

- Perform a SPOC analysis—Identifying Strengths, Possible Improvements, Opportunities & Challenges (2 hours)

- Gap analysis—identify the gap between where you are now versus where you want to be (2 hours)

- Define your organizational Goals, Objectives & Strategies (4 to 8 hours)

- Establish your organizational Action Plans (4 to 8 hours)

- Present your strategic plan at an all-employee, company-wide meeting(s) with opportunities for questions and answers (2 hours per presentation)

- Cascade the Goals, Objectives, Strategies & Action Plans down to the departments (8 to 16 hours per department)

For your consideration, following are some common strategic planning formats I have used with clients and which have proven successful for their unique situations:

Format 1 (Warp Speed):
One continuous retreat

A Native American enterprise with more than 1,000 employees chose to complete their strategic plan in the shortest timeframe possible. They wanted to get everyone involved, on the same page, and moving in the same direction as quickly as possible. Here's how I assisted them to do it.

On Day 1, we met with Tribal leaders and the enterprise's Senior Management Team to develop the purpose, values, mission and vision.

Then on Day 2, senior and middle managers met to review and refine input received during Day 1. They performed the SPOC Analysis and developed goals, objectives, and strategies.

On Day 3, senior managers, middle managers, and other important team members reviewed and refined input gathered during the first two days and began developing the Action Plans for each goal.

Then, during the week following the three-day organizational retreat, I spent a day with the team members of each department— cascading the organizational plan down through the organization— guiding them to complete their own departmental strategic plans.

After all departments had completed their plans, they held company-wide meetings with each shift to present the strategic plan and receive input.

Here are the advantages and disadvantages of the Warp Speed approach:

- **Pros** – Gets everyone on the same page quickly; Most economical approach, especially if you are paying for the services of an outside facilitator and his/her travel expenses.

- **Cons** – May be difficult to get all participants to commit to the entire process; May need more time to research certain aspects before committing to implement the results.

Format 2 (Super Charged):
Two separate retreats,
followed by independent work by departments

A construction company with 75 employees chose to bring their leaders up to a retreat center in the mountains to begin their strategic plan. They expanded the employee involvement to include a second retreat. Here's how I assisted this group:

The leaders traveled to the retreat location, arriving mid-day on Friday, staying overnight, and departing mid-day on Sunday. I incorporated some fun teambuilding activities and exercises throughout the weekend in order to help break up the intensity of the many planning sessions. Because people stayed overnight, it allowed us to pack in many diverse exercises that stimulated their thinking and caused them to connect at a deeper level.

On Day 1, senior management attended. I guided them to create Declarations of Understanding, followed by a teambuilding exercise and the drafting of the organizational Purpose and Values.

On Day 2, middle management joined with senior management. We began with a teambuilding exercise and then completed their Purpose, Values, Mission, and Vision, and began looking at future trends. The day ended with a celebration party. (Note to self: consumption of alcohol by participants makes for a slow, tough start the following morning.)

On Day 3, we completed a SWOT (which I now refer to as SPOC) analysis to assess the organization's strengths, weaknesses, opportunities, and threats. This was followed by drafting Goals, Objectives, and Strategies.

One week later, a one-day retreat was held expanding employee involvement in order to complete the Goals, Objectives, and Strategies and begin working on the Action Plans.

Their department leaders then worked with their direct reports to complete the departmental Action Plans.

I suggest that if you choose a format like this one, don't let more than two weeks elapse between the two retreats because you'll want to keep the momentum growing.

Here are the advantages and disadvantages of the Super-Charged approach:

- **Pros** – Gets the plan completed and gets people on the same page in a reasonable amount of time; People have more time to digest the information and research key aspects.

- **Cons** – Delays completion; Life happens, and participants may miss the second round of sessions because of dealing with personal issues that have arisen; The facilitator will need first to review the progress with the group in order to get everyone back up to speed.

Format 3 (4th Gear):
Hold 4 or 5 one-day retreats,
plus work group follow-up

A board of directors and a leadership staff representing twenty-five member agencies chose to space four sessions over the span of three months. The board members also own and operate their own agencies, so they were not able to dedicate four consecutive days to their strategic plan. Here's how I assisted them:

During the first session, we identified their Purpose and Values, and updated their Mission, reviewed their existing Vision, performed a SPOC analysis (identified Strengths, Possible improvements, Opportunities and Challenges), and began creating their Declarations of Understanding.

During the second session, we completed their Declarations of Understanding, the Circle of Success Assessment, expanded Vision, identified Goal Areas, and began developing Goals, Objectives and Strategies.

During the third session, we finalized and prioritized their Goals, Objectives and Strategies, and began developing Action Plans for each goal.

During the fourth session, we invited other member agency owners to join Work Groups that were established to complete the Action Plans for each goal. The leaders spent several hours working with team members to make progress developing their assigned Action Plans.

The Work Groups continued to meet independently after the fourth session to complete the Action Plans.

Here are the advantages and disadvantages of the 4th Gear approach:

- **Pros** – Takes bite-sized pieces of time in the participants' work week; Gives people even more time to digest information before moving to the next segments.

- **Cons** – People's enthusiasm may diminish from week to week; Because of many starts and stops, a great deal of information has to be rehashed in order to remind people of what has been accomplished and why; Could result in an even higher monetary investment in the facilitator as well as the investment of travel time for participants.

Format 4 (Cruising Speed):
Hold a dozen half-day retreats,
plus Action Team assignments

A Native American community comprised of a Tribal Council, approximately 1,200 government employees, and 10,000 Community Members chose to create their strategic plan over the span of six months to ensure that everyone was in alignment. Here's how I worked with them:

First, we created a Steering Committee, which was made up of several members of the Tribal Council, the Community Manager, and approximately ten other senior executives.

The Steering Committee was responsible for creating or refining a draft of the Purpose, Values, Mission, Vision, Goals, Objectives, and Strategies for review and approval by the Tribal Council. Meetings were held weekly and bi-weekly to whittle away on completing the elements.

Then, Action Teams were established to create Action Plans for each goal. Other government employees, Community Members, and Council Members were invited to participate. Everyone involved was invited to an Action Team launch luncheon and work session to hear a presentation of the strategic plan elements and to kick off the Action Planning process.

Meetings were held with each Action Team to assist them with understanding their assignment and moving in the right direction.

A comprehensive communication plan was established to inform all stakeholders of the results and status of the process. Strategic plan presentations were made to each department director and at Council meetings. A series of articles was published in their Community newspaper to inform the Community Members of the results of the process.

I suggest that you not allow too much time to pass between sessions, because this tends to stifle the momentum. You may wish to hold at least one planning session per week.

Here are the advantages and disadvantages of the Cruising Speed approach:

- **Pros** – Less non-billable time per week per employee; Participants are able to put in some work time in the office even during planning days; Participants have a great deal of time to research and digest the information.

- **Cons** – Could experience a significant reduction in enthusiasm; More opportunities for participants to miss sessions; Significant rehashing of information; The process can be drawn out for many months; Most expensive format of the scenarios with regard to participant time and facilitator costs.

Format 5 (Start-up): Planning sessions for partners with few employees

Two co-owners of a relatively new business with just a few employees decided that it was time to create a strategic plan. They decided to start a business together because they were good friends who worked well together and loved their line of work. Their business was expanding, but they didn't have the infrastructure or clarity to support the expansion. Here's the way I supported their growth:

We met in a coffee shop for a series of two-hour coaching/planning sessions. During each session, I helped them work on one or two of the key elements. At the end of each session, I gave the partners homework to finish what we had started that day or to prepare to work on the next key element to be discussed during our upcoming session.

We were able to complete their strategic plan within six sessions; and as it so happened, just two months after completing their plan, a huge opportunity came their way which would double the size of their agency! Because they were well prepared and organized, they had the ability and confidence to seize the opportunity.

- **Pros** – Coaching/planning sessions are most appropriate for one or two people; Much can be accomplished within the two-hour window of meeting time; Homework can fill in the gaps; Participant(s) can space the monetary investment over a longer period of time.

- **Cons** – Could complete the plan sooner by means of a one- or two-day retreat (It's certainly better to have a plan *before* you launch a new business or deal with an expansion.)

Questions and considerations
to help determine the format

1. By when do you want to have the strategic plan completed?

2. Who do you want to include in the strategic planning process?

3. How much time can be devoted to each session?

4. Schedule the sessions so that the strategic plan can be completed on time and involve the right people.

5. Communicate the objectives of the strategic planning process to the participants and ask them to commit to attending by placing the sessions on their calendars.

3) Send the Right Message

Dale Carnegie said, "There is only one way . . . to get anybody to do anything. And that is by making the other person want to do it."

Here's how you can make your employees want to be included in the strategic planning process.

At the beginning of the planning process, it is a good idea to develop a communication plan that identifies all the stakeholders and outlines how you will communicate with them.

In your initial communication to your employees, let them know that participating in the strategic planning process is a great honor and privilege. Also, share with them how important the strategic planning process is to the enduring success of the organization and how important their input is to the direction of *their* company—in the end, it really does matter what they think, say, and do.

Here are some general pointers about communication:

Before the strategic plan begins

- Couch your communications in the form of a very persuasive invitation (not a mandatory edict)
- Use email as a tool to follow up with participants but not as the sole method of communication (Remember that people are bombarded by emails these days.)
- Consider personally inviting the key players
- Craft all communication with an energetic, positive tone
- Enroll people in being part of the new direction and vision of the organization
- Talk it up in every meeting, genuinely reemphasizing the importance of honest, candid communication and employee input in the strategic planning process

During the planning sessions

- Thank people for participating
- Create an atmosphere of trust and openness
- Be encouraging

- Keep communication focused on the topic at hand (minimize tangents)
- Follow the communication plan to keep all stakeholders informed about progress
- Send out emails to those not in attendance to share what was accomplished and what their role will be
- Establish an Eagle Team to keep the plan alive and the communication flowing

Follow-up communication after the plan is complete

- Invite all employees to a company-wide meeting(s) to learn about the completed strategic plan, and give them the opportunity to ask questions and provide comments
- Announce the formation and role of the Eagle Team
- Email the strategic planning results to every employee (or have them available on a shared computer drive)
- Write a series of newsletter articles to highlight various elements of the plan
- Display strategic plan results in high-traffic employee areas
- Assign employees to Action Teams
- Create individual development plans (IDPs) for all employees

Throughout all your communication, envision that you are creating a ball of productive energy, much like stoking the fires in the furnace of a power plant.

4) Create the Right Atmosphere

Howard Schultz, CEO of Starbucks said, "You walk into a retail store, whatever it is, and if there's a sense of entertainment and excitement and electricity, you wanna be there."

People walking into your planning sessions, should feel electricity in the air and want to be there, similar to the experience of walking into a Starbucks store.

The environment can make or break the strategic planning process.

Minimize distractions as best you can. If your budget allows, I have found it to be highly desirable to hold your retreat offsite at a hotel or other venue that is relatively quiet and secluded.

50 Group Facilitation Secrets
I've Learned During My Career

In my 25 years as a facilitator, trainer, instructor, speaker and coach, I have learned many secrets to engage groups. Here are 50 for you to consider:

Insights gained as a TLC Master Facilitator and Trainer . . .

1. Remember that your participants are the stars—let them do 80 to 90% of the talking. You can fill in the remainder.

2. Don't be afraid of a little chaos—it's a natural part of the process, and order and agreement will eventually appear.

3. Check your ego at the door.

4. Don't take things personally—people are never upset for the reasons you think.

5. Everyone has a valuable piece of the puzzle to contribute.

6. It's easier to be a facilitator if you love people.

7. Be a spherical thinker—see everyone's viewpoint (opinion) as a valid point on a sphere.

8. Search for the unspoken message hidden beneath the words.

9. Trust your intuition to know the perfect questions to ask and the right exercises to use to help the group progress

10. Engage people's hearts and minds—lasting transformation occurs only when the heart is involved.

11. Hold their attention—present information using a variety of ways in which people learn best (e.g., visual, auditory, kinesthetic, creative, analytical).

12. Meet the members of the group at their present level of consciousness and strive to lift them to a higher level.

13. Look for opportunities to WOW!—make the experience unique and memorable.

14. Be patient and let the process unfold naturally, rather than trying to force it.

15. Be compassionate and empathetic when emotional situations arise.

16. Hold the confidences as sacred—just like Las Vegas, "What's said in the room stays in the room."

17. Maintain the delicate balance between achieving results and allowing time for dialogue.

18. A smile and a little appropriate humor go a long way toward lightening up tense situations.

19. You don't have to be the content expert; instead, draw out from the participants their innate wisdom.

20. Enjoy the process!

. . . insights gained as a Dale Carnegie instructor . . .

21. Arrive at the room early enough in order to get everything set up and ready to go before the first participant appears.

22. Welcome each participant as he or she enters the room.

23. Keep everything organized and professional-looking (i.e., chairs orderly, supply table neat, posters straight).

24. When you begin, engage the participants within the first 60 seconds.

25. Keep the energy moving and building; don't let the momentum drop.

26. Mix it up—keep things interesting and fresh by varying the exercises and by occasionally springing surprises upon your audience.

27. Dress just above the level of the best-dressed person in the room.

28. Build up a reserve of information—be ready with 100 times the amount of information than you can possibly share in the allotted time.

. . . insights gained as a corporate trainer and facilitator . . .

29. Develop clear objectives about what is to be accomplished.

30. Always have a clear agenda.

31. Test well in advance all equipment that will be used.

32. Create professional-looking guidebooks and other handout materials.

33. Deliver what you've promised (or reach consensus to do otherwise).

34. Use appropriate room set-ups for different purposes
    - Theater/auditorium style for information-sharing
    - U-shape for whole-group discussions
    - Breakout tables or chairs in circles for small group activities

35. Comfortable chairs are a must. Our butts can take only so much. Getting people up frequently to do voting or to participate in discussions can also help.

36. If you want to ensure that everyone shows up on time, bring food and they will come. Have any meals and refreshments be light, with low carbohydrates that provide sustained energy.

Avoid foods containing high doses of sugar, because they will eventually produce a downward spiral in one's energy.

37. Select a room with plenty of wall space on which to tape completed flipchart pages. I love to wallpaper the room with the participants' good work. Hang everything the group creates so they can see the progress they are making. It also makes their input easily accessible when you want to refer to key decisions that have been made. When I was an engineering project manager, I would take over a conference room that I could use as a Situation Room, leaving our work up until it was completed (especially when choosing to use a lengthy strategic planning format). It's also a marvelous way for your employees to review the progress being made.

38. Keep the room in an orderly fashion, especially at the beginning of the session when people are arriving. Neatly laying out handouts, Post-it notes, Sharpie Markers, etc., communicates the subtle message that you care.

39. Keep PowerPoint slides simple, using few words and nothing smaller than a 24-point font size. Remember also that a picture is worth a thousand words.

40. Choose the perfect venue in which people will feel special and where there will be minimal distractions.

41. Make the environment an inviting, multi-sensory experience. Put everything in its place. Pay attention to every little detail (i.e., bring in fresh plants, make every chair line up perfectly, vacuum the floor if necessary, use air freshener or sage, control the temperature, and vary the lighting appropriately for each exercise).

42. Be sure that the room is well lit. Natural lighting is best. Incandescent light bulbs are more effective than florescent bulbs for sustaining participants' energy levels.

43. Play nice, uplifting and energizing music before sessions as participants are arriving, during breaks, and in the background during exercises. It's amazing how music can revitalize a room.

44. Purposefully focus the energy by arranging everyone's chair to face the facilitator.

45. Ask participants to turn their phones off or on silent whenever the strategic planning sessions are occurring. If at all possible, request that participants use their technology only during breaks.

. . . insights gained from my Native American friends and clients . . .

46. (Okay, this part may seem a little "woo" to you, but just notice how you feel when you think about it.) To cleanse the area of residual negative energies, you may want to smudge the room with sage or do a simple blessing to set a positive energy in the room for the people who will join together. Native Americans do this ancient practice whenever they gather together.

47. If you will be doing an exercise in which you want everyone's input, consider using a "talking stick" that is passed from person to person, providing everyone with an equal opportunity to speak.

. . . insights gained as a trained mediator . . .

48. Seek common ground—look for common threads, interests and agreements.

49. Give everyone an equal opportunity to be heard.

50. Focus attention on finding solutions to issues, rather than concentrating on the personalities involved.

Enjoy employing these secrets to hone your own facilitation skills.

In a nutshell, here is how I like to create the right atmosphere:

1. Find the perfect venue and room in which to facilitate the process. Comfortable chairs and good, adjustable lighting are a must. Reserve the room, make arrangements for audio-visual equipment, and order refreshments. Make sure the room reservation is scheduled to start at least two hours prior to the time the participants will arrive, so you can do any fine-tuning of the setup.

2. If possible, visit the room personally before making the reservation in order to ensure that it will serve your needs. Make sure it has sufficient wall space to post flipchart pages. It's better to be prepared than to be (unpleasantly) surprised.

3. Arrive several hours before each session to assure the proper room set-up and to test the audio-visual equipment. Have you noticed that technology doesn't always cooperate? Arriving early helps reduce stress and frustration during those troubleshooting times. Also, make sure you pack all the cables and connectors you will need even if the venue staff thinks they have what you need. Learn how to operate the lights and control the air conditioner if necessary.

4. Be impeccable with neatly setting out everything you will need. An organized room minimizes distractions and feels inviting.

5. Play appropriate, uplifting music as people enter the room.

6. Be sure that all your slides, documents, and handouts are ready to go so as to minimize timing glitches and assure smooth transitions.

7. Make the room as inviting and comfortable as possible.

Energizing Thoughts to Ponder for Chapter 15

1. When do you want to complete your strategic plan?

2. What format (or combination) do you prefer for your organization?

3. Who do you want to involve in the various sessions?

4. What are the best ways to invite your strategic planning participants?

5. What are the best ways to communicate results and status reports company-wide?

6. Who is the best person on your leadership team at crafting inspiring, persuasive communications?

7. What venue would contain the least distractions and provide the greatest energy?

8. How can you assure that everyone arrives on time?

9. How can you ensure that your employees temporarily assign their job responsibilities to someone else during the time they will be participating in strategic planning sessions?

Chapter 16

Facilitating the Strategic Planning Elements

"Efficiency is doing things right.
Effectiveness is doing the right things."

~Peter Drucker
Management consultant, educator, and author of 39 books
including *The Effective Executive*

Engaging participants using storyboarding

This final chapter provides my step-by-step formula for orchestrating an engaging, enjoyable, and productive strategic planning process.

You will be guided to complete successfully each element of the process that I have described in previous chapters.

1) Performing the Circle of Success Assessment

(Refer to Chapter 1 and See Appendix C for worksheet.)

The Circle of Success is a simple assessment tool that will enable you and your employees to see at a glance the "flat spots" in your organization as well as the areas in which you are maximizing your potential. See Figure 17. I consider it an organizational medicine wheel.

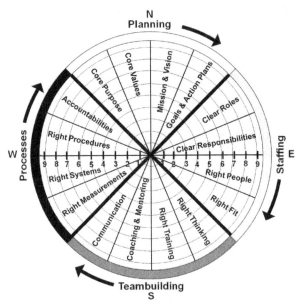

Figure 17: Circle of Success Assessment Tool (revisited)

I have been using this simple, yet revealing strategic planning tool for many years when I work with the organizations I serve. It provides leaders, like you, with a quick visual assessment of many of the ingredients that generate success and profitability in organizations. It's also a remarkable, engaging teambuilding exercise. Here's how it works:

1. You'll notice that there are four quadrants in this wheel: (1) Planning; (2) Staffing; (3) Teambuilding; (4) Processes. Each quadrant has 4-sectors, or focus areas, (in which to invest energy and resources)—a total of 16 focus areas to assess.

2. Superimposed on the Circle of Success is a horizontal scale identified by 10 concentric circles with zero ("0") in the center and "10" on the outer circumference.

3. Here's how it works: First, decide what you want to assess— the organization as a whole or any individual department you choose. Invite your leaders to do the same to see how your collective points-of-view align or differ.

4. Now it's time to score how you think/feel your organization is doing. The scoring works like this: Zero ("0") is the lowest score and indicates that your organization or department is performing poorly in that particular area. Ten ("10") means your organization or department is functioning in an exemplary manner in that particular area and couldn't do better if you tried.

5. Score each sector separately by asking yourself, "At this point in time, how well has our organization (or department) defined, communicated and performed in this particular area?" (As a first step, you can score each sector on the "Circle of Success Matrix" included in Appendix C if you desire.) For each sector, put an "X" on the scale in the center of the wedge you are scoring.

6. When you have scored all 16 sectors, connect the dots. (See the example on the next page in Figure 18.)

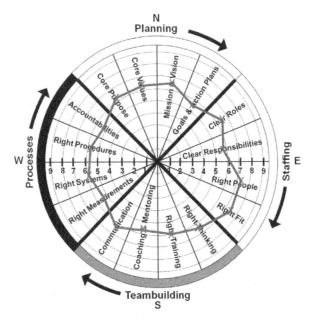

Figure 18: Example of completed Circle of Success Assessment

7. Now look at the "wheel" of connected dots you have just created. Would the "wheel" roll? Do you happen to see any interesting shapes? (Similar to looking for shapes in cloud formations, some of my perceptive clients have enjoyed identifying shapes resembling birds, bells, and other outrageous images. Have fun with it!)

8. Compare your wheel with others who have joined you in doing this exercise. Discuss the similarities and differences.

9. Now identify low, "flat spots" on the wheel that need attention. These are notable areas in which to set goals and invest resources, maximizing your potential by bringing those areas back into alignment and balance.

10. Use this tool at least quarterly to see how well your organization (or department) is progressing. There will always be new sectors of your organization that need attention because organizations are living, breathing organisms constantly ebbing, flowing, and morphing.

It's your turn now. Give it a try. I think you'll like its simplicity and effectiveness.

2) Identifying Your Core Purpose

(Refer to Chapter 2 and see Appendix C for worksheet.)

Here's a fun and inspiring way to facilitate a Core Purpose session:

I love to facilitate this process using the ingenious method of storyboarding, which incorporates flipcharts, different-colored Post-It Notes, and black Sharpie Markers. Storyboarding, used extensively by Walt Disney, is the same process movie makers use to create a motion picture. Similarly, it works quite well for planning purposes.

Senior managers are usually the people who create the Core Purpose, because they are the closest to understanding the "Big why?" the organization was formed. The session for this element typically lasts approximately two hours if your team hasn't attempted to define it previously.

Here's how I like to facilitate the process:

1. Set up two or three flipcharts on easels at the front of the room, each with "Core Purpose" written at the top.

2. Distribute different-colored pads of Post-It Notes and black Sharpie Markers to all participants. "Why use different colors?" you may ask. Color stimulates the brain and, as

a side benefit, beautifies the room. Additionally, I enjoy watching participants barter with each other to acquire their favorite color.

3. Explain how storyboarding as a tool works and give the following instructions:

   a) All ideas are valid; there are no silly ideas.

   b) Speak your idea before writing it, so everyone can hear it and no one else duplicates it.

   c) Write only one idea per Post-It Note, using the black Sharpie Marker. You can have as many ideas as you want, but put them each on separate Post-Its.

   d) Hold up your Post-It as soon as you complete it so the facilitator can collect it and put it on a flipchart for all to see. Do this repeatedly until all members of the group have exhausted their ideas on the topic. Posting the colorful sticky notes on flipcharts gives everyone immediate feedback on the progress being made and helps to assure that ideas are not duplicated.

4. Ask the group this question: "Why are you here in the world as a company?" In other words, "Why does your company exist?" This is the core reason why the organization was created initially (besides just making money), and this is the same core reason why its existence will continue.

5. Make sure everyone participates—even the quiet ones. One of the greatest benefits of storyboarding is that all participants can share their ideas, even though some may be reluctant to speak. If you have individuals who choose not to speak, you can, nevertheless, collect their written input to place on the flipcharts.

6. Distribute "smiley face" or "star" stickers (something fun) to all the participants. My "Rule of Thumb" for determining how many stickers to distribute to each person is 10-20% of

the total number of ideas displayed on Post-It notes on the flipcharts. Next, invite everyone to come up to the flipchart(s) and vote for their favorite ideas, using only one sticker per Post-It note (This prevents loading or skewing the voting). This is the "exercise" part of the program. Getting people up from their chairs and moving around from time to time keeps them energized.

7. When everyone has completed voting by means of stickers, reorder the Post-It Notes on the flipcharts, placing at the top those Post-Its that receive the greatest number of sticker votes.

8. Encourage the group to suggest various Core Purpose statements, based on the top vote-getter Post-Its placed at the top of the flipcharts until you reach an "Ah ha... that's it!" moment. Remember that the final Core Purpose statement should be something very simple, yet empowering—the essence, or core, of why your company exists. It should make your heart sing.

9. Write the completed Core Purpose statement on a flipchart and tape the chart up on the wall, along with the flipcharts containing the raw Post-It Note input. Keep all the raw input, because these can provide valuable ideas for creating your values and mission statements.

10. After the session, type all the input, noting the number of votes each idea received. Distribute the document to the appropriate people the following day if possible. These ideas will most likely be referred to later.

11. After senior managers have drafted the Core Purpose, let middle managers review and comment on it to enhance its clarity, but not change its essence.

3) Defining Your Core Values

(Refer to Chapter 3 and see Appendix C for worksheet.)

Akin to the Core Purpose session, I love to facilitate the Core Values process using the storyboarding method, which employs flipcharts, different colored Post-It Notes, and black Sharpie Markers.

I like to begin this work with senior managers of the organization. Once they have created the initial list of Core Values, I like to keep the values in draft form, resembling moldable clay, while I work with them to gather input from middle management levels, then frontline supervisors, and then the remainder of the employees of the organization. The initial session with Senior Management to define the values lasts approximately two hours. Subsequent groups in the hierarchy require less and less time to refine those values.

Here's how I facilitate the Core Values session if a company has never identified its values:

1. Set up six flipcharts on easels at the front of the room, each with "Values" written at the top as a header. (Note: Based on my experience, I have seen that organizations typically

identify between four and seven core values, although there is no magic number.)

2. Distribute pads of different-colored Post-It Notes and black Sharpie Markers to all participants.

3. If I haven't done it in a previous session with the group, I explain how storyboarding works and give the following instructions:

   a) All ideas are valid; there are no stupid ideas.

   b) Speak your idea before writing it, so everyone can hear it and no one else duplicates it.

   c) Write only one idea per Post-It Note, using the black Sharpie Marker. You can have as many ideas as you want, but put them each on separate Post-Its.

   d) Hold up your Post-It as soon as you complete it so the facilitator can collect it and put it on a flipchart for all to see. Do this repeatedly until all members of the group have exhausted their ideas on the topic. Posting the colorful sticky-notes on flipcharts gives everyone immediate feedback on the progress being made and helps to assure that ideas are not duplicated.

4. Begin by asking the question, "How do you like to be treated?" (You'll never go wrong referencing "The Golden Rule," which exists in some form in every culture.) Another revealing question you could ask is, "What do you choose to stand for as a company?" Here's even another: "What do you want to be known for (your legacy)?" Each question adds a slightly different dimension to the answers you'll receive. Asking a question in different ways helps to keep the ideas and energy flowing.

5. Make sure everyone participates—even the quiet ones. One of the greatest benefits of storyboarding is that all participants can share their ideas, even though some may be reluctant

to speak. If you have individuals who choose not to speak, you can, nevertheless, collect their written input to place on the flipcharts.

6. When all ideas have been captured on Post-It Notes and randomly stuck on flipcharts, invite four to six people who like to assemble puzzles to come up to the front of the room, instructing them to cluster the ideas written on the Post-Its into common themes or groupings.

7. Then, ask this same work group that is standing at the flipcharts to think of a title for each cluster or grouping. From my experience, there are usually four to seven overreaching values that rise to the top. Direct the work group to distribute those clusters among the six flipcharts, which will give them plenty of room to organize their groupings.

8. After the small work group has completed its work, encourage the entire group to comment upon and tweak the organization of the groupings. Assess whether or not any of the groupings actually are a subset of another overreaching value and, consequently, need to be moved to the correct position.

9. Distribute "smiley face" or "star" stickers (something fun) to all the participants. My "Rule of Thumb" for determining how many stickers to distribute to each person is 10-20% of the total number of ideas displayed on Post-It notes on the flipcharts. Next, invite everyone to come up to the flipchart(s) and vote for their favorite ideas, using only one sticker per Post-It note (This prevents loading or skewing the voting). This is the "exercise" part of the program. Getting people up from their chairs and moving around from time to time keeps them energized. When everyone has completed voting by means of stickers, reorder the Post-It Notes within each cluster on the flipcharts, placing at the top those Post-Its that receive the greatest number of sticker votes. Announce to the entire group the top vote-getters under each Value grouping.

10. Form small groups of two to four people, and assign each small group one value to begin with. You can have fun organizing this activity by asking, "Who wants Value (insert title)?" The first small group member who raises a hand, claims that value for their group. Continue doing this process for each value until all groups have been assigned a value.

11. Charge each small group with the task of writing a clarifying statement or definition of the assigned value, using the input received on the Post-It Notes for that value. (Instruct them to use as many top vote-getters as is feasible). To help in accomplishing this assignment, distribute a box of Scented Markers to each small group and give instructions to write on a separate flipchart the value statement/definition (double spaced so it can be edited easily). "Why use scented markers?" you ask. Because they're fun, they smell good, and they are not toxic. (Note: I love watching adults as they sniff the markers and try to guess the flavor. Just a word of caution: Some enthusiastic sniffers come away with colored dots on their noses as a result (it can be quite entertaining!)

12. If there are any Value sheets that remain unassigned, give the opportunity to the first group that finishes its first assignment to choose an additional Value sheet on which to work. Continue assigning remaining Value sheets until all have been completed.

13. Solicit a representative from each group to read the Value statement/definition, explaining how the top vote-getters were incorporated.

14. Next, invite the members of the entire group to provide feedback. Have them begin by sharing first what they like. Then, let them share what changes they would suggest. Lead any further discussion and/or voting on suggested changes, modifying the statement/definition of each Value until everyone agrees, "That's it!"

15. When each Value statement is completed, celebrate by using a shortened version of the parliamentarian process:

"All those in favor, say 'Aye!'... all those opposed, 'Nay!'... Motion carried unanimously!" Place a big checkmark on the flipchart, and lead the group in applause. The idea is to keep it fun and lively.

16. Plaster the walls with the completed Values flipcharts.

17. Follow the same reporting and editing process until all groups and all values have been finalized and accepted.

18. For added fun and amusement, investigate with the group to see if there is a memorable acronym that can be derived from the first letters of the Values. For example, several years ago, I facilitated this process with a leadership group at Phoenix-Mesa Gateway Airport (formerly Williams Gateway Airport); and after completing their values, the following acronym had emerged: "S.P.I.R.I.T." In my subsequent trainings and coaching with those leaders, we had great fun devising ways to implement and integrate their S.P.I.R.I.T. values into everything they did.

19. Solicit input from all areas of the organization by having middle managers review and suggest refinements. Then, in a cascading fashion, do the same review with frontline supervisors and, finally, with all employees. It is especially important that Core Values gain everyone's buy-in and support, because Values are the desired day-to-day behaviors expected from every employee in the company.

20. Finally, ceremoniously adopt the final values; and plaster the walls with them in every nook and cranny where employees gather.

21. Keep the Core Values alive in every company communication and activity.

4) **Crafting Your Mission Statement**

(Refer to Chapter 4 and see Appendix C for worksheet.)

Completing a mission statement usually requires approximately two to three hours—that is, as long as this element follows Purpose and Values sessions; because the raw input already gathered usually contains the ingredients for formulating a good mission statement. Otherwise, it most likely will take longer.

Begin by enlisting senior and middle managers to draft the mission statement. Next, solicit feedback and input from frontline supervisors until you reach agreement. Then, communicate the mission statement to the masses.

Here's how I facilitate the creation of a Mission Statement:

1. Review the questions that contribute to developing a Mission Statement, and inform the participants that they have already answered the first two questions during the sessions devoted to completing the Core Values and Core Purpose. As I mentioned in Chapter 4, the questions are as follows:

   a) *How do you choose for people to behave? (most important core values)*

b) *Why is your organization here?; why does it exist? (core purpose; the heart of your mission statement)*

c) *What does your organization do? (products and services you provide)*

d) *What results do you desire for your organization? (beyond monetary gain)*

e) *Who does your organization serve? (your customers)*

2. Form small groups of three or four people to draft possible mission statements that include the answers to all these questions, using as a priority the input from the Purpose and Values exercises.

3. Instruct each group to write the draft of a mission statement on a lined flipchart. (Let participants use scented markers and double-space the writing so it can be refined more easily). Ask them to tape their completed flipchart on the wall next to other groups' mission statements so that all flipcharts can be compared.

4. Allow people to vote for what they think are the most significant words and phrases displayed in each draft mission statement. After gathering this input, I underline the words and phrases they identified.

5. Combine the phrases they liked best into a new Mission Statement, and continue to hone it until you arrive at a unanimous, "That's it!" Then applaud everyone's success.

6. Solicit feedback and input from frontline supervisors. Like clay, keep molding the Mission Statement until you reach agreement on the final form.

7. Similar to the Values process, ceremoniously adopt the Mission Statement and plaster the walls with it in every nook and cranny where employees gather.

8. Keep the Mission alive in every company communication and activity.

5) Establishing Your Vision

(Refer to Chapter 5 and see Appendix C for worksheet.)

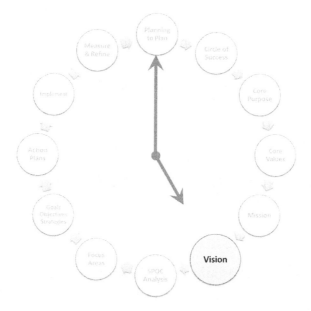

The visioning process typically takes approximately two to four hours to complete, depending upon the level of detail the organization chooses. However, it should be noted that if you plan to solicit input from a large Community using a multiple number of focus groups, the process can be a much longer time commitment.

Here's how I facilitate the visioning process with small to mid-sized companies:

In general, begin the process with senior and middle managers. Next, seek feedback and input from frontline supervisors. Finally, share it with all employees.

Here's how I like to facilitate the visioning process:

1. Before everyone arrives for the session, plaster a wall with numerous (4 to 6) blank sheets of flipchart paper butted up against each other such that there appears to be one long, solid piece of paper. Draw a timeline that extends from the

date of conception of the organization to five or ten years into the future (whatever your preference). Make the timeline scale spaced out enough to accommodate multiple rows of Post-It Notes above each year.

2. Invite everyone to come up to the timeline on the wall (the "exercise" part of the program), Post-It Notes and Sharpie Markers in hand, to post what they remember as the company's key events or milestones achieved from its inception to today. This activity gives a powerful historical picture of what has been accomplished together as a company. It causes everyone to feel good about the collective progress. (I find that a visual representation of everything that the company has accomplished gives people a feeling of appreciation and pride about how far they have come together.)

3. (Optional: For progressive, heart-centered groups, I lead them through a guided visualization with eyes closed, and invite them to imagine the organization in its perfect working order ten years into the future. I ask them to see themselves floating above the company's facility and peering with x-ray vision into the building in order to observe what's happening—i.e., what's happening with staff, customers, the facilities, activities, products, and services. This has proven to be a powerful exercise for enlightened teams.)

4. Seated back in their chairs, participants brainstorm and write on Post-It Notes their ideas of what they would love to see for the company in the future—taking note of the year in which they envision it. Stick their Post-It Notes on the appropriate year on the timeline. Continue this exercise until all ideas have been collected.

5. Lead a discussion about the possibilities identified by everyone for the future desired state of the organization. Get everyone back up to the timeline on the wall, and start them working together to move the Post-Its around to various years until everyone is in agreement about the picture of the future.

6. Give everyone ten smiley stickers to place on the ten Post-Its, representing future possibilities thought to be most important for the success of the organization. This task helps to prioritize what is most important to the collective group and gives some indications of where to focus the company's energy and resources. The Post-It Notes with the greatest number of stickers are most likely the areas or projects suitable for setting goals.

7. Lead the group to create an overreaching statement that identifies what the organization can be the best at in the world (or at least in their locale). This becomes the employees' aspiration of what can be achieved together—their collective Vision Statement; it is the mind and heart expanding and stretching to new heights; it is their collective greatness emerging.

8. Type all the input into the format of a matrix timeline that will make it easy to see the progression.

9. Senior and middle managers will solicit feedback and input from frontline supervisors, followed by communicating to employees the new vision/direction.

6) Performing Your SPOC Analysis

(Refer to Chapter 6 and see Appendix C for worksheets.)

Performing a SPOC Analysis necessitates approximately one or two hours per group, which includes time for hearty discussion.

I begin by meeting with senior and middle managers to do a SPOC Analysis for the organization. In addition, more often than not, I will guide the managers to do the same analysis for their departments with their direct reports.

Here's how I facilitate the process:

1. Prepare four flipcharts with the following headings: "Strengths," "Possible Improvements," "Opportunities," and "Challenges."

2. Using Post-It Notes to record answers, participants focus on each one of the following questions (as discussed in a previous chapter):

   a. "What are the *Strengths* of the organization?" These are the areas in which your organization does well, in which you excel. Capitalize on these strengths, and your organization will prosper, your teams will maximize their potential, and your employees will be productive and fulfilled.

b. "What *Possible Improvements* would help your organization to be more successful?" These are areas in which you may presently be experiencing some deficiencies. What improvements will help your organization achieve the Core Purpose, Core Values, Mission, and Vision more quickly and effectively? These deficiencies impede progress like traffic speed bumps, slowing your progress. (Hint: Look back at the "flat spots" that appear on the wheel of your Circle of Success Assessment covered in Chapter 1. These particular areas need some sort of improvement.)

c. "What potential *Opportunities* could you seize that will move your organization closer to accomplishing its mission and vision?" These ideas are most likely unexplored activities and projects or untapped knowledge and skill-building events. These opportunities are represented by the stars that fall within your Cone of Influence, as discussed in Chapter 7. Taking advantage of these opportunities will accelerate your progress toward success.

d. "What *Challenges* might you need to overcome?" Consider your challenges as obstacles, or roadblocks, standing in the way of achieving success. Some of these could even be showstoppers for you and your company. Like water that flows along a rocky stream, you will need to find creative solutions in order to make your way over, around, or through these obstacles in order to realize your Mission and Vision.

I encourage participants to share as many ideas as they can. When they have exhausted ideas for one section, move on to the next until all questions are answered.

3. Keep things lively and moving quickly. This is a "snap" session, not a time for in-depth discussion. Just capture as many ideas as possible. Five minutes per question is usually sufficient time.

4. Let everyone independently select what they feel are the top five (most significant) ideas on each flipchart by putting smiley face stickers on the Post-It Notes. Here are some questions to consider as they perform this exercise:

   a. For the "Strengths" flipchart: "What are our most important strengths that we can leverage and apply to a greater extent in order to effectively and efficiently achieve our Purpose, Values, Mission, and Vision?"

   b. For the "Possible Improvements" flipchart: "What do we need to improve upon in order to achieve our Purpose, Values, Mission, and Vision?"

   c. For the "Opportunities" flipchart: "What opportunities should we focus energy and resources upon that will help us to achieve our Purpose, Values, Mission, and Vision?"

   d. For the "Challenges" flipchart: "What possible challenges are most important for us to overcome in order to achieve our Purpose, Values, Mission, and Vision?"

5. When everyone has finished voting, move the top-priority Post-it Notes (the ones with the greatest number of stickers) to the top of the charts; and conduct a lively discussion about the areas that are most important upon which to focus energy and devote resources. You will most likely see some key themes emerge. These will, in all probability, be the best areas in which to set organizational goals.

6. This type of analysis is a great soul-searching exercise to do with each department as well.

7) Explaining the Cone of Influence for Focusing Your Energy

(Refer to Chapter 7)

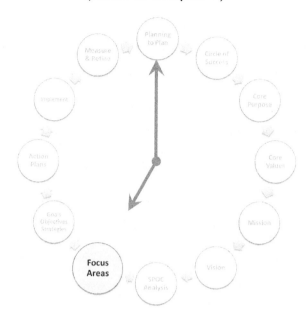

How I like to facilitate understanding the "Cone of Influence"

I give this ten-minute overview for each separate group that joins the strategic planning process.

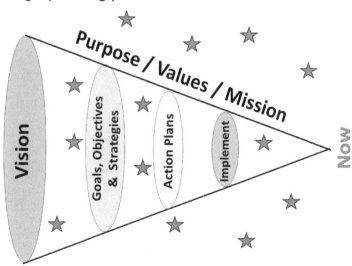

Figure 19: Cone of Influence (revisited)

1. Ask, "When making decisions regarding opportunities, do you know when to say 'yes' and when to say 'no'?"

2. Define the "Cone of Influence" as a tool whose boundaries are represented by your organization's Purpose, Values, Mission, and Vision. Any opportunity that lies inside the Cone of Influence is one on which to expend resources because it is in alignment with what is important to your organization. You could say 'yes' to that opportunity. For any opportunity that lies outside the Cone of Influence, you should say 'no' without any hesitation. (The only exception is when your organization expands your Mission or Vision).

3. Explain that, once you have defined your "Cone", all the organization's Goals, Objectives, Strategies, and Action Plans should move the company closer to achieving its Vision and Mission and living its Core Values.

8) Developing Your Goals, Objectives, and Strategies

(Refer to Chapter 8 and see Appendix C for worksheet.)

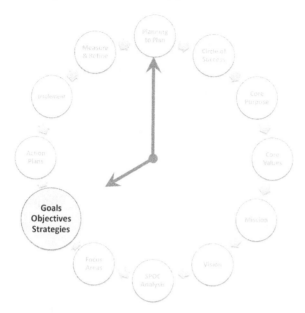

How I like to facilitate the process

This process can last between four and eight hours, depending on the loftiness of the goals.

I begin the process with senior and middle managers. Next, receive feedback and input from frontline supervisors. Then, communicate to all employees. Finally, every employee is assigned to one or more of the goals.

Here is how I facilitate these elements:

1. Review the S.M.A.R.T. W.A.Y. of structuring goals, which was discussed in Chapter 8. As a refresher, here it is:

   - **Specific** (not too vague),

   - **Measurable** (so you know the progress you're making),

   - **Attainable** (reachable but causes one to stretch to achieve it),

- **Relevant** (in alignment with your purpose, values, mission and vision), and...

- **Time-bound** (scheduled milestones). It is also important that you have your goals be...

- **Written** (this makes them more solid), and build in...

- **Accountability** (hence, the need for individual development plans for your employees); and, finally, possess a strong...

- **Yearning to achieve them** (Never underestimate the power of enthusiasm!)

2. Review the priorities you identified during the SPOC Analysis.

3. Review the priority input received during the Visioning session.

4. Identify important "Themes" or "Goal Focus Areas" in which to set goals. (I suggest you identify no more than five; otherwise, you probably will find yourself feeling overwhelmed.)

5. Ask the participants what Goals would be best to focus on for each of the Themes. Conduct an open and specific discussion about where best to apply your resources. Reach consensus as a group, or at least democratically vote on participants' preferences of Goals on which to focus.

6. Home in on one or two goals under each Goal Focus Area, and write those on the corresponding flipchart.

7. Break the participants into small groups and assign to each group a Goal Focus Area with its suggested goals. It is best to assign people who have a passion and the knowledge, skills, and experience necessary to refine the details for each Goal Focus Area.

8. Have each team identify possible objectives and the strategies to accomplish each Goal.

9. Designate a representative from each small group to present to the entire group their recommended draft objectives and strategies for each Goal.

10. Guide the entire group to offer refinements to the recommendations from the small groups until consensus is reached.

11. Meet with frontline supervisors to continue the refining process.

9) Creating Your Action Plans

(Refer to Chapter 9 and see Appendix C for worksheet.)

How I like to facilitate the process:

Typically this part of the process requires at least two sessions (8 to 16 hours total) to complete, depending on the complexity of the goals. It could take longer if additional research or input is necessary to define the plans fully. Many times, I work with upper-level and middle management to create the framework, and then on the following day, invite frontline supervisors and other subject-matter experts to add their input, especially regarding Tactics and other specifics about which only frontline employees would have the best knowledge and current experience.

Here are the steps I use:

1. Establish a Strategic Plan Steering Committee that will establish and oversee the progress of Action Teams charged with creating Action Plans for each Goal Focus Area.

2. Establish Action Teams for each Goal Focus Area. Involve people from different levels in the organization with the right knowledge, skills, and experience so that you get high-quality,

relevant input and support and buy-in for implementing the Goals.

3. For each Action Team, assign a team leader whose responsibility will be to work with the team to complete the assigned Action Plan.

4. Using either Post-It Notes or the mind mapping process, each Action Team will identify tactics or tasks for each strategy created. I actually use mind mapping software into which I load everyone's input so they can see the results on a big screen. I then tweak the plans as I receive feedback from other groups. It's a really cool and engaging process, because people can see the "big picture" form right before their eyes.

5. After they have completed their mind maps, each Action Team completes an Action Plan spreadsheet for the assigned Goal Focus Area by filling in the blanks related to tasks, schedule, and resources required to complete each task.

6. Each Action Team provides regular progress reports to the Strategic Plan Steering Committee until all assignments have been completed to the satisfaction of the Committee.

10) Implementing Your Action Plans

(Refer to Chapter 10 and 11)

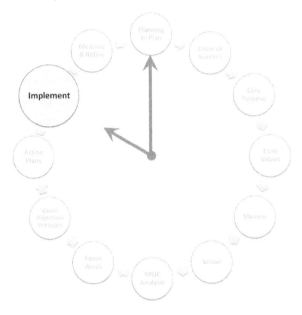

Establishing an Eagle Team

How I like to facilitate the process:

1. Create an Eagle Team, made up of people from all levels of the organization, whose job it is to be on the constant lookout to discover energizing, fresh ways to keep the strategic plan alive and show acknowledgment or appreciation to those making great contributions to its success.

2. At least once per month, hold a teambuilding energizer that reinforces some aspect of your values, mission, or vision.

3. Dedicate a section of your monthly newsletter to report progress on the strategic plan and to acknowledge key individuals (a different person every time). If you don't have a newsletter, create another form of monthly communication.

4. Create, or follow, your communication plan to update all stakeholders on the organization's progress.

5. Keep celebrating significant milestones!

6. Look for every opportunity to show appreciation. A simple handwritten thank-you note or card goes a long way and costs little.

Orchestrating the O.W.N.E.R.S.H.I.P. Puzzle Exercise

How I like to facilitate the process:

Here is an impressive, fun exercise I like to use when I talk about the topic of ownership. I use an actual 108-piece puzzle of the earth and separate the puzzle into 5 sections (if I have 5 groups, for example). I like to use the earth puzzle because it's recognizable to all and symbolizes that we are all connected. Here's how I proceed:

1. Separate each of the five sections (one for each group) into individual pieces and put each section into its own plastic Ziploc bag. Distribute the bags of individual puzzle pieces to each group, giving the participants only one rule: "Use good judgment." Let them figure out what to do. It takes very little time for them to discover that they need to put their own puzzle section together first, then join their section with the other groups' sections until the puzzle has been completed. Lead a debriefing session about what "taking ownership" means and the resultant behaviors that showed up during the exercise. Finally, help them relate the game experience to their organization and its strategic plan.

2. Once you have assigned everyone a "piece of the puzzle" from the strategic plan (so that employees have a vested interest in accomplishing the goals), include those goals in their Individual Development Plans. Their "piece of the puzzle" now becomes part of their performance review.

3. Assist each leader in your organization to create a Declaration of Understanding (DOU) with each of his/her direct reports. This declaration is a list of behaviors designed to set the framework on which each person can count on the other. The first part of the list forms the "common ground" that works in a reciprocal fashion—leader to direct report and direct report to leader. The second part outlines what the leader desires and expects of his/her direct report and what the direct report desires and expects of his/her leader.

4. Meet at least quarterly to assess progress being made on Individual Development Plan goals and DOUs.

11) **Measuring and Refining**

(Refer to Chapters 12 and 13)

Measuring – Measure Your Progress

How I like to facilitate the process:

1. Identify the important areas to measure in your company.

2. Identify at least one measurement for each Goal, Objective, and Strategy you identified in your Action Plan.

3. If you don't already have a system in place to monitor the area you want to measure, build one. Remember, it can be low-tech or high-tech.

4. Identify how you plan to monitor progress on all your Goals, Objectives, and Strategies.

Refining – Ebb and Flow with Conditions

How I like to facilitate the process:

1. Communicate clearly to all stakeholders any changes that may, or will be, occurring. It's always good to minimize surprises.

2. When your organization is facing significant internal and external changes, perform another SPOC Analysis. This time when assessing your company's Strengths, Possible Improvements, Opportunities, and Challenges, focus on determining your organization's ability to deal successfully with the change.

3. Communicate to the Steering Committee about working with the Action Teams to modify the Goals, Objectives, Strategies, and Action Plans in order to deal with the ensuing change.

4. Inform everyone of the modifications being made to the plan.

5. If necessary, modify employees' Individual Development Plans.

Appendix

Appendix A: Glossary of Terms

Appendix B: The 5 Essential Focal Points of Great Leaders

Appendix C: Strategic Planning Forms

Appendix D: Example of a Credo

Appendix A

Glossary of Strategic Planning Terms

Planning – A formal, systematic ongoing process for making decisions to bring about a desired future state.

Strategic Planning – The process of examining the entire organization in the environment in which it exists. It incorporates all levels of planning: services, budgeting, and operations.

Core Values – The desired behaviors and underlying "guiding principles" of how decisions are to be made by each person in the organization.

Core Purpose & Mission – Clear and concise statements that answer respectively the following questions: "Why are you here?" and "What business are you in or about?"

Vision – A statement that paints a vivid picture of the desired future state of the organization.

SPOC Analysis – Environmental Scan

- History and major trends
- **S**trengths and **P**ossible Improvements
- **O**pportunities and **C**hallenges

Gap – The difference between the present state of the organization and the desired future state (Purpose, Values, Mission, and Vision).

Goals – Typically, goals are broad statements of intention. A goal is defined as a broad aim toward which your efforts are directed. It's a "what," not a "how." In other words, it tells you where you are going rather than how you will get there. Goals should be consistent and in alignment with the Purpose, Values, and Mission and move the organization toward its Vision.

Objectives – Objectives are closely tied to goals. And the two terms are often used interchangeably—but Goals and Objectives are different. An Objective is a specific and measurable milestone that must be achieved in order to reach a Goal. Each Goal may include several Objectives.

Strategies – A Strategy is a way to achieve an Objective. Strategies tell you how you're going to get there, the overall direction you are going to take. Each Objective may include several Strategies.

Tactics – A Tactic is a specific action step required to deliver on a Strategy. Tactics are what you do; and for every Strategy, there are a number of Tactics.

Implementation – The phase of strategic planning that involves taking action, monitoring progress, making mid-course corrections and updating the plan if necessary due to unforeseen circumstances.

Appendix B

The 5 Essential Focal
Points of Great Leaders

These 5 Essential Focal Points of Great Leaders have been integrated into the chapters of this book. The strategic planning process will provide you an excellent framework for implementing them.

Great leaders care as much about the growth of their people as they do about the bottom-line—those leaders constantly strive to build high-performing teams while also encouraging individual fulfillment.

Paraphrasing from Jim Collins and Jerry Porras, in their bestselling business book *Built to Last*, in great organizations everyone knows exactly what needs to be done and when to do it. Like gears in a precision-made clock, everyone's part synchronizes perfectly with everyone else's. If someone is absent or having a bad day, like clockwork someone else steps up without missing a beat—without excuses, without ego.

It's easy to see what greatness looks like in the sports and entertainment industries, since they are so visible and are studied relentlessly under a microscope. We saw it with Brian Epstein and The Beatles 50 years ago. We saw it in 2014's Super Bowl blowout with Pete Carrol and the Seattle Seahawks. We saw it with Bob Brenly and the 2001 World Series-winning Arizona Diamondbacks. More than see it, we feel it!

Figure 20: Five Essential Focal Points of Great Leaders

Here are 5 essential focal points of great leaders in great organizations:

Aspiration – Great leaders aspire to achieve lofty visions and have their employees and organizations "be the best they can be." They generate a high level of 'Team Spirit.' The highest aspiration for any organization is to have the entire team performing such that they almost move together as one unit in pursuit of a mutual goal.

Assessment – Great leaders assess the present situation to determine the best path forward. They continuously monitor employees and customers to better understand their ever-changing desires and expectations—always looking for ways to increase their level of satisfaction and fulfillment. They are also skillful predictors of their competition's next move.

Alignment – Great Leaders create alignment and support from the top of the organization to the front-line. They strive to get everyone focused and moving in the same direction, toward the same vision, demonstrating the same behavioral values.

Accountability – Great leaders coach employees to live their agreements. They create a culture of personal responsibility and accountability such that employees understand the level of performance that is expected of them. Great leaders understand that anyone who chooses not to fulfill their agreements will probably be happier somewhere else, and they help them to see that.

Acknowledgment – Great leaders catch people in the act of doing things right. They build a culture of celebration and appreciation while improving the quality and depth of communication, strengthening relationships, and building trust.

Appendix C

Strategic Planning Forms

- Circle of Success Matrix Assessment

- Circle of Success

- Declaration of Understanding

- Core Values

- Core Purpose and Mission

- Vision

- SPOC Analysis

    o Strengths and Possible Improvements

    o Opportunities and Challenges

- Gap Analysis

- Goals

- Objectives, Strategies & Tactics

- Action Plan Submittal

For a link to download the free Strategic Planning Guidebook with these forms, see the '**Free Resources**' section at the back of this book.

CIRCLE OF SUCCESS MATRIX ASSESSMENT

Instructions: Rate your present level of success in each of the key sectors identified below that contributes to the prosperity of your organization. A ten (10) indicates that you are effective and efficient in that area and couldn't be more successful if you tried. A zero (0) indicates that your organization is performing extremely poorly in that area and couldn't do worse if you tried.

Key Sectors	Rating (0 to10)
PLANNING	
Core Purpose: You have a written core purpose that identifies why your organization exists—your employees understand it and factor it into the heart of their decisions and actions.	
Core Values: You have a set of written core values that guide employees' behaviors and how they treat each other and your customers. They are promoted and enforced consistently.	
Mission & Vision: You have a written mission statement that clearly defines your business, and a vivid vision of your desired future state that provides your employees clear direction.	
Goals & Action Plans: You have identified in writing the goals, objectives, strategies, tactics, schedules, and resources required to achieve your purpose, mission, vision, and values.	
STAFFING	
Clear Roles: Your employees understand their unique roles in the organization—their piece of the puzzle—and how their roles are important to the success of the organization.	
Clear Responsibilities: Your employees understand their job duties and responsibilities and their bosses' desires and expectations of them so they can be successful.	
Right People: You have hired the right people who possess the necessary attitude, skills, and knowledge for the organization to be successful and for them to be fulfilled.	
Right Fit: You have placed your employees in the right jobs that match their talents, skills, abilities, and passions to maximize their potential and optimize their contribution.	
TEAM BUILDING	
Right Thinking: Your employees make good, confident decisions— with minimum supervision— that are in the best interest of the organization, customers, and their team.	
Right Training: You provide employees with the necessary training for them to develop the right attitude, skills, and knowledge to perform their jobs effectively and efficiently.	
Coaching & Mentoring: You provide employees with coaching and mentoring developmental opportunities to help them reach their goals and achieve success.	
Communication: Communication flows effectively and efficiently throughout the organization such that employees are kept informed and given ample opportunity for feedback.	
PROCESSES	
Right Measurements: Progress is measured so that it is always clear how well things are going toward fulfilling the values, mission, vision, goals, objectives, strategies, and tactics.	
Right Systems: Required systems (high-tech & low-tech) are established to make the goals, objectives, strategies, and tactics operational and deliverable—effectively and efficiently.	
Right Procedures: Procedures are identified in writing for effectively and efficiently accomplishing the different processes in the different departments.	
Accountabilities: Employees understand their commitments and responsibilities and are encouraged to be self-accountable—supervision holds them accountable if necessary.	

CIRCLE OF SUCCESS

Maximizing Alignment and Performance

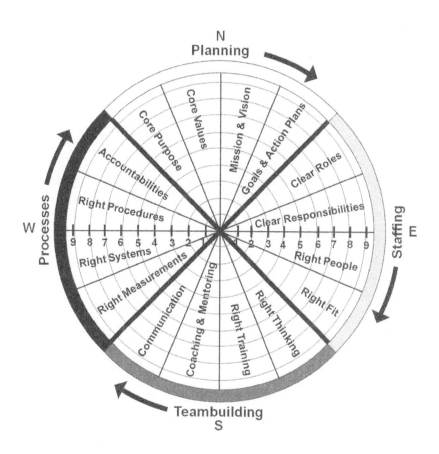

DECLARATION OF UNDERSTANDING ™

_____ **desires and expectations of**

_____

Our "Common Ground":		
How we choose to treat each other...What we can count on each other for...		
1.		
2.		
3.		
4.		
5.		
6.		
7.		
_____ desires and expectations of _____ performance...		
1.		
2.		
3.		
4.		
5.		
6.		
7.		

Signatures:

_____ _____ _____

_____ _____ _____

Date: _____

CORE VALUES

What behavioral values are important in the decisions made by people representing or serving your organization?

Values are your governing principles and qualities that are your organization's highest priority. Your organization's value system consists of the standards and principles upon which individuals and departments base their decisions and actions. Values form the foundation, support and direction for your decisions. In essence, they are the compass for your choices.

Value	Description

CORE PURPOSE & MISSION

1. Describe what you understand your organization's present purpose and mission to be.

2. List any questions, ideas, or concerns you have about the present mission.

3. What might be the best mission for your organization now and in the future? It should answer the following questions:
    A. How do you choose to have people behave (*Values*)?
    B. Why is your organization here? – Why does it exist? (*Purpose*)?
    C. What does your organization do (important *Roles* or *Services*)?
    D. What *Results* do you choose your organization to have?
    E. Who does your organization serve?

Present Mission

Concerns with the Present Mission

New Mission

VISION

What is your vision of the organization in its desired future state?

Write a statement or description of what you see. It may include:

Technical skills	Staffing	Finances
Systems	Facilities	Marketing/Sales
Services	Allies	Clients/Customers
Results achieved	Others	

Present Vision

Concerns with the Present Vision

New Vision

STRENGTHS & POSSIBLE IMPROVEMENTS

1. List the major <u>strengths</u> and <u>possible improvements</u> of your organization.
2. Identify which strengths and possible improvements will be most critical to your organization's future success?

Strengths	Possible Improvements

OPPORTUNITIES & CHALLENGES

1. List the major <u>opportunities</u> and <u>challenges</u> your organization will face in the next 1 to 3 years.

2. Identify the opportunities and challenges that are most critical to your organization's future success.

3. Opportunities and challenges may be assessed in the following areas:

Technical skills	Staffing	Finances
Systems	Facilities	Marketing/Sales
Services	Economy	Competitors
Allies	Organizations/agencies	Other?

Opportunities	Challenges

GAP ANALYSIS

What are the gaps that exist between the present state and the desired future state?

Gaps are discrepancies between the organization's desired future state (values, vision, purpose and mission) and its present performance. These discrepancies or differences of potential are where the organization's goals and action plans should be focused. This is a reality check. It is here it must be decided whether the gap is too wide to bridge considering the limit of available resources during the planning horizon. If the gap is too large, the vision and mission may need to be modified accordingly.

Present State	Desired Future State

GOALS

1. Review the values, purpose, mission, vision, strengths, possible improvements, opportunities, and challenges.

2. List as many possible goals as you can think of. A goal is a broad statement of what you intend to do.
3. Prioritize goals in order of importance to the organization.
   A = Imperative: Must be achieved to achieve your organization's desired future state.
   B = Important: Will enhance your organization but you can achieve your desired future
   state without it
   C = Low: Will have no effect on reaching your organization's desired future state.

Goal	Priority (A, B or C)

OBJECTIVES, STRATEGIES & TACTICS

Goal ___: _____

Leader(s): _____   _____

Objectives	Strategies	Tactics
Objective A:	Strategy 1:	Tactic 1:
		Tactic 2:
		Tactic 3:
	Strategy 2:	Tactic 1:
		Tactic 2:
		Tactic 3:
	Strategy 3:	Tactic 1:
		Tactic 2:
		Tactic 3:
Objective B:	Strategy 1:	Tactic 1:
		Tactic 2:
		Tactic 3:
	Strategy 2:	Tactic 1:
		Tactic 2:
		Tactic 3:
	Strategy 3:	Tactic 1:
		Tactic 2:
		Tactic 3:

Action Plan Submittal
_____Strategic Plan

Date: _____
Goal: _____
Submitted By: _____ (Action Team Leader)

Action Team:

Executive Summary of Recommendations:

Objectives	Strategies	Tactics	Priority (A, B, C)	Start Date	Due Date	Budget ($)

Measurement of Success: Key Performance Indicator(s) (KPIs)

Appendix D

Example of a Credo

Phoenix-Mesa Gateway Airport Authority
(Formerly Williams Gateway Airport Authority)
Created by Lynn Kusy, former Executive Director

We are a group of people who have come together and exist as an institution we call Williams Gateway Airport Authority so that we are able to accomplish things collectively that we could not accomplish separately—we make a contribution to the community—a phrase which may sound trite, but which is fundamental.

Our mission is to plan, organize, and direct the provision of superior airport facilities and services to the aviation community and the public in a safe and efficient manner. The people that make up the organization are critical to the success of that mission. It takes people operating, maintaining, and managing the Airport in a superior fashion in order for us to accomplish our mission.

We must create an environment of trust, an environment in which each individual trusts the other members of the team to carry their weight, perform their job and to support the rest of the group. That means we place our trust in individuals and we place our trust in the organization itself.

There are certain reasons why each of us has chosen to work here. Those reasons must align with our mission statement and our SPIRIT values. The Airport Authority's full mission statement includes our SPIRIT values, namely, Safety, Pride, Innovation, Responsibility, Integrity, and Talk-It-Out. The SPIRIT values are the foundation on which this credo is based and are the value system which should be adopted by each employee. In fact, we use the SPIRIT values to screen prospective employees during the interview process. They are used in our individual performance management evaluations. And they are integral to the way we act with and toward each other every day.

The Airport Authority's purpose statement identifies innovation and public service as keys to our reason for being. Community service is a basic element of this credo. Each employee is here because of his or her desire to serve the public. Community service can take many forms. In this organization it means economic development and the running of a public airport. In our personal lives, it might mean service to community organizations, religious organizations, or other groups within the community. It is important that each of us balance our work life with our family life and understand the contribution that we make to our family.

Our underlying drive comes largely from the desire to serve— generally to do something which is of value to all. The real reason we are here, the reason for our existence, is that we provide something which is unique, something that makes a contribution to the community—to the world. Individual willingness to be of service to others will manifest itself in an organization that goes out of its way to do the things that are asked of it and even the things that no one asks it to do.

The other key word in our purpose statement is innovation. We approach tasks creatively, not doing things the same old way, but looking for new ways to tackle old jobs and asking new questions, such as, "What should we change?" and "What else do we want to accomplish?" Personal resourcefulness, tapping into the sources of energy and support available in the organization and in the community, is critical to our success. We also display openness toward diverse ideas, experiences, people, and ways of doing things.

Profit must be a cornerstone of what we do—it is a measure of our contribution and ultimately a means of self-financed growth— but it is not the point in and of itself. The point, in fact, is to create a win-win outcome, and winning is judged in the eyes of the customer and by doing something we can be proud of. There is a symmetry of logic in this. If we provide real satisfaction to real customers, we will be profitable.

When our personal values align with the values of the organization, our employees will enjoy coming to work and find ways to have fun at work. We also want to help the community have fun when they come to the Airport by providing a place where fun is inherent in the experience. We want students, customers, employees, and pilots to enjoy the experience on every occasion.

In summary, we can create an environment of trust, where we trust the individuals and trust the organization, where we fully support each other and understand the reasons why we are here. As a result, our organization accomplishes its mission, supports its purpose, and lives its SPIRIT values. Working together, having fun, and undertaking outstanding accomplishments are the result of living our mission and purpose statements and living our SPIRIT values every day, at home, at the office, and in the community.

About the Author

Ray Madaghiele is the Chief Inspiration Officer and Master Facilitator of Business Energizers, a division of the Transformational Learning Center (TLC), an organizational and human excellence company, whose purpose is to inspire hope and awaken greatness in individuals, organizations, and communities.

Ray has more than 25 years' experience facilitating, training, speaking and coaching in organizations and communities across the United States. His engaging processes and proven principles inspire people to "get clear, get organized, get going, and get results."

Some of his clients include engineering companies, utilities, municipalities, airports, land developers, construction companies, and Native American communities and their enterprises. He guides leaders to create an energized, fulfilling environment where individuals and teams grow and thrive.

Ray's facilitation specialties include strategic planning, leadership retreats, community visioning, problem solving, and employee engagement focus groups. His engaging and interactive facilitative style draws out and captures participants' best ideas in a remarkably short period of time.

His customized training and speaking specialties focus on leadership, teambuilding, strategic planning, goal setting, customer service, creative problem solving, effective communications, human relations, project management, and time management.

His leadership success coaching assists leaders to accelerate the implementation of facilitation and training outcomes in their organizations and in their personal and professional lives.

Ray's company, Transformational Learning Center (TLC), won the Gilbert, Arizona, 2001 Community Excellence Award for Small Businesses. Ray also won the 1999 Community Excellence Mayoral Award for his work in leading Gilbert's Community with Character initiative, and facilitating various community leadership forums. Ray also served as a board member and facilitator for the Arizona Character Education Foundation and the Gilbert Leadership Program.

Ray earned a B.S.E. in Civil Engineering and worked 10 years as a civil engineering project manager for several consulting firms and a large utility where he led multi-million dollar planning, design, and construction projects.

Ray expanded his education by taking graduate studies in learning and instruction, and classes in facilitation, mediation, project management, leadership, and personal and organizational strategic planning.

While an engineer, he became a certified Dale Carnegie Course Instructor and taught classes in effective communication and human relations for 8 years.

Ray is also author of the book, *Ray of Hope: Inspiring Peace – Insights on Chaos and Consciousness while Bicycling Across America*. This inspiring book chronicles his 3,369 mile, 70-day bicycle ride from Phoenix, AZ, to Ground Zero, NYC, in the aftermath of the 9-11-01 events. In it, he shares timeless principles for achieving greater peace and happiness in our lives, our communities, and the world.

The cycling journey served as a stepping stone for Ray and wife Lyn's new RVing adventure. They now serve their business clients' needs flexibly and economically while they travel across North America living their dreams—and inspiring others to live their dreams also.

Contact Ray

Contact Ray through his interactive website, by phone, on social media, or by mail at:

Transformational Learning Center
3916 N. Potsdam Ave., Suite 3946
Sioux Falls, SD 57104

Phone: 480-495-7152
Fax: 480-632-1303

Website: www.BusinessEnergizers.net

LinkedIn: https://www.linkedin.com/in/raymadaghiele

Facebook: https://www.facebook.com/businessenergizers

Free Resources

FREE Strategic Planning Guidebook Companion to *Energize Your Business*

To receive your FREE 8 1/2" x 11" *Energize Your Business Strategic Planning Guidebook*, go to
www.EnergizeYourBusiness.info

Service Corps of Retired Executives (SCORE) – SCORE is a nonprofit association dedicated to helping small businesses get off the ground, grow and achieve their goals through education and mentorship.
https://www.score.org

U.S. Small Business Administration (SBA) – The SBA helps Americans start, build and grow their businesses. SBA operates Small Business Development Centers (SBDCs) throughout the United States.
http://www.sba.gov

SPECIAL NOTE: A percentage of all book sales is being donated to the SCORE Foundation to support small business success in America.

Ray's Resources and Services

Group Facilitation

Our facilitation specialties include strategic planning, leadership retreats, community visioning, problem solving, and employee engagement focus groups. Our engaging and interactive facilitative style draws out and captures participants' best ideas in a remarkably short period of time.

Leadership Development Training and Workshops

Our customized training and speaking specialties include leadership, teambuilding, strategic planning, goal setting, customer service, creative problem solving, effective communications, human relations, project management, and time management.

Leadership Success Coaching

Our leadership success coaching assists leaders to accelerate the effective and efficient implementation of facilitation and training outcomes in their organizations and in their personal and professional lives.

Facilitator Train-the-Trainer Certification Program

Our master facilitators offer an onsite train-the-trainer program to develop your internal facilitators' skills so they can masterfully guide your internal strategic planning process using tools outlined in this book.

Contact Ray by email at Ray@BusinessEnergizers.net to schedule a complimentary needs analysis and inquire about which of his services can best fit your organizational needs. Also, we would love to hear your comments about the value you have received from this book and the success you have achieved by applying its principles.

Enjoy an Excerpt from
Ray's Previous Book...

Ray of Hope: Inspiring Peace

Insights on Chaos and Consciousness While Bicycling Across America

By

Ray Madaghiele

Table of Contents

IT'S TIME!

By Ray Madaghiele
2:00 a.m. September 15, 2001

It's time that we understand our role as stewards of this planet –

That we respect and honor the delicate balance of our world.

It's time that we realize, "We are all one people" –

That separateness is an illusion and that, in truth, we are all connected.

It's time that we see past the veil of illusion called separateness,
and understand just how connected we really are –

That we are all made from the same substance of the universe,
and by harming another we are only harming ourselves.

It's time we see past the color of one's skin or the name of one's God –

That we realize we are merely traveling parallel paths leading up the same mountain.

It's time that we stop searching for happiness outside ourselves –

That we turn our attention inward and tune in to the calm peace of our souls.

It's time, if we see something in the world that needs to be changed,

That we do as Gandhi suggested, "Be the change you wish to see."

It's time that we take responsibility for making the world a better place –

That we strengthen the foundation of our communities by being of good character.

It's time that we ask, "How can I make a difference?" –

That we leave this world in a little better shape than when we arrived.

It's time that we listen to each other with empathy and compassion –

That we overcome the fear in our minds so that we can experience the love in our
hearts.

It's time that we get past ego and discover our innate spiritual essence –

That we release our selfish desires and serve humankind unconditionally, with love.

It's time that we "Love all, serve all" –

That we be at peace.

IT'S TIME!

(For a free downloadable version of the It's Time! poem, visit
www.RayofHopeInspiringPeace.com)

Preface

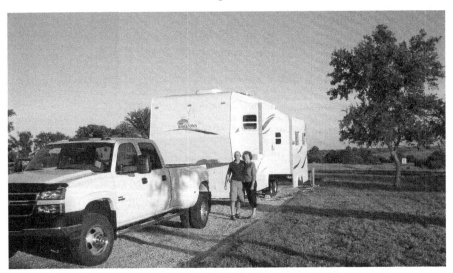

**Lyn and Ray in Kansas on the first day
in their new "Madaghiele Mansion"**

Video Link: http://www.youtube.com/watch?v=Tzo8UGiCh4Q

I can't believe it's been ten years since I pedaled my bicycle across America in the wake of the September 11, 2001, terrorist attacks that shook the foundation of our peace. My wife, Lyn, and I were inspired to deliver a message of hope and healing, and we chose as our way of doing that to play a version of leap frog across the country— with me on the bike and her in the support vehicle, a 1991 Toyota 4Runner filled to the brim with baggage. As we rolled, we connected with thousands of kindred souls in town after town. It turned out that many of those folks were also inspired to be rays of hope and light, serving humanity in their own unique ways. Clearly, the events and significance of 9/11 struck an emotional chord in everyone.

Ray of Hope: Inspiring Peace honors the sacred stories people entrusted us with, and it reveals timeless principles that can help each of us be more peaceful and joyful no matter what is happening in our lives and the world. Many people have shared with me that the first edition of this book helped them to muster the courage and be motivated to act on their own inspired ideas.

With all the chaos that has surfaced in the world since my 2002 Cycling for Peace journey and the first edition of this book, you might be surprised at all the positive, productive, restorative and uplifting ideas and initiatives that have emerged. This book includes highlights of the incredible positive transformation that has occurred during the past ten years and that is continuing to unfold in the midst of today's economic, political and societal turmoil.

The 2002 Cycling for Peace journey transformed Lyn and me. When I pedaled the last stroke of the journey and we made our way into New York City on September 10, 2002, you would think I would have been exhausted and glad it was over, right? Mission accomplished! Now I can rest and recuperate. But that was not the case. Instead, we didn't want to stop. We felt that we should keep going—to continue the adventure and to connect with more people.

"But weren't you homesick?" some asked. As we had begun this adventure we thought we might be, but we were not. Yes, I missed my boys, our friends and clients, but not our house or possessions. I believe now, that in those few short months, we discovered and lived the true meaning of, "Home is where the heart is."

Here was another interesting discovery: We had packed our Toyota 4Runner with everything we thought we would require for our 80-day trip from Phoenix to Ground Zero, NYC. We packed too much! Much of the baggage we lugged with us was never used. What an epiphany! We learned that we do not need many possessions to live well and be happy.

As Lyn and I reminisced about our trip on our drive home from New York to Arizona, we realized that we shared similar feelings—a sense that there was more to do.

The first few months after returning home, we enjoyed reconnecting with familiar faces. Many organizations and schools asked us to tell the story of our journey and reveal the lessons we had learned. I was humbled by the overwhelming interest. It prompted me to write *Ray of*

Hope for Peace, mainly to share the experience with my inner circle.

Still, an empty feeling persisted. What was it? Surely not to keep bicycling! But we definitely missed the adventure, the mesmerizing sound of tires on pavement, and the joys of discovering beautiful vistas, meeting interesting people, and making new friends.

Then we began a hearty dialogue with our friends Kay and Tom, who had been criss-crossing North America fulltime in a Recreational Vehicle (RV) for over ten years. They frequently shared pictures of the beautiful sights they had encountered and told delightful stories of interesting people they had met. They owned the kinds of businesses that allowed them to be mobile. No longer did they feel the need to plant permanent, deep roots in any one locale. North America became their backyard. They were free to roam about the country at will. Their lifestyle intrigued us.

The Cycling for Peace journey offered us a taste of what Kay and Tom were experiencing, and as the result, their dream lifestyle became our dream.

As we began planning to make the conversion to a more adventuresome lifestyle, it became incredibly apparent that all the "stuff" we had collected over our lifetimes was really nothing more than a burden we had been carrying from place to place. All that "stuff" was anchoring us and limiting our freedom. It was time to lighten the load. We made a radical, yet logical, decision to simplify our lives. We began releasing unneeded possessions and downsizing our living space. Anything not used within the past two years was sold or donated. Well, almost anything.

I must admit that it wasn't easy to part with some things—especially those with sentimental value. They held fond memories and had emotional links to significant times in our lives. We decided to store our photos, significant books and important papers in an eight-by-eight storage unit for future access. To help my boys cope with our changing lifestyle, we gave them the opportunity to take anything they desired back to their mom's place. But every stick of furniture, all appliances, most artwork and all our knickknacks found loving new homes with appreciative friends (known and unknown).

As an engineer, I had learned that plans are meant to evolve as circumstances change. That insight became very useful. A friend of mine, who knew of our RVing dream, alerted us in April of 2006, "If you plan to sell your home you better do it now. The economy is about to take a dive into a deep recession."

"But we are planning to wait until the kids graduate from high school before RVing," I said. Yet a voice deep inside me knew he was right and prompted me to act on his guidance.

Our house was listed and sold before the Arizona housing market collapsed. Happily, I had acted on my friend's wisdom. I trusted that same wee, small voice within that had also told me in 2001 to cycle across America.

The Cycling for Peace adventure transformed our understanding of what is truly important to our sense of peace, happiness, and success. It became a stepping stone to our new RV adventure.

While renting a smaller, temporary home we worked with an RV manufacturer to design and build an RV that would fulfill both our personal and business needs. Our businesses are of the nature that, through the miracle of technology, they can be operated as we roll.

One of the most difficult decisions to make involved our 14-year-old cat, Ozzie. Do we take him on the road with us or find him a new home? It takes a special cat to endure the many hours of travel in a rumbling diesel pick-up truck with a fifth wheel in tow. As it turned out, he loves travelling with us! Ozzie really enjoys a good passenger-side lap during a full-day of travel. He has even become more social and talkative with all the new people we meet.

A new chapter in life began.

Nowadays, as we explore the beauty of North America in our RV, we continue to share an inspiring message of hope with everyone we meet. It surprises us that not many people seem to dig beneath the fear-provoking mainstream news to discover the many positive things that are happening in many sectors of society.

Today, as in 2002, people have a deep yearning to be involved in encouraging discussions that inspire hope in the midst of chaotic events. I have realized how important it is to our collective well-being for everyone to be a "ray of hope" to their circle of family, friends and associates. Such an attitude, with its positive behaviors, literally radiates ripples of energy of peace, love and joy out to our communities, then to our nations, then around the whole world.

A great deal of positive transformation is occurring, even though it is not generally reported through mass media outlets. Just surf the worldwide web, as I do—with the intention of finding positive, inspiring information—and I am certain you will discover many wondrous innovations and engaging initiatives. Like a geothermal vent, much is bubbling beneath the surface, ready to be tapped and channeled to create powerful outcomes.

The final chapter of this book highlights examples of some of the positive, constructive initiatives that are emerging to improve our world.

My hope is that, by studying and practicing the principles revealed in this book, your wellbeing will flow more abundantly to you and through you, causing you to be a brighter, more courageous "ray of hope" and light for all to see.

Introduction

From Phoenix, AZ, to Ground Zero, NYC
July 4 - September 11, 2002

CYCLING FOR PEACE

Contact: Ray Mastagnvak
480.526.0588
Raymg@ILClevdesigz.com

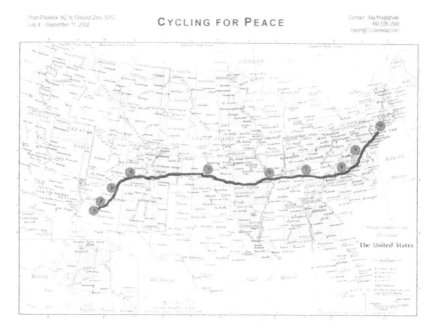

**Map of the Cycling for Peace route with
locations of Fire Station Chats.**

With all the chaos in the world today, how can we possibly have peace of mind? I answered that question for myself and then shared it in a unique way with thousands of people across America.

For the seven months since I received the vision, the journey has been just an idea—an intangible dream. Now it was beginning to feel real. It was 6:10 am, July 4, 2002, and already 100 degrees in downtown Phoenix, Arizona. My wife, Lyn, and I walked up the sidewalk toward the stairs leading to the Phoenix Civic Plaza. As we made it around the building, we could see a crowd of about thirty people gathered for our send-off.

As we climbed the steps onto the plaza to greet those who had come to support us, a local television news reporter pulled us aside. Camera rolling, the reporter teed up our interview, "We are at the Civic Plaza in Phoenix on this 4th of July where a Valley man and his wife are about to begin a unique trip across America. Ray is going to bicycle over 3,000 miles in 70 days from Phoenix to Ground Zero, New York City, to arrive in time for the year anniversary of the September 11th terrorist attacks on the World Trade Center. Lyn will be joining him, following in a support vehicle." The reporter turned to me and asked, "Why have you decided to take on such a feat?"

I told him, "As a result of the 9-11 events, there are so many positive lessons that we all have learned about how to treat each other. We need to remember what we learned and keep building on the positives. With the ensuing war on terrorism, I felt the need to share a message of possibility across the United States. We will be holding public seminars in fire stations across the nation to honor the public servants who modeled exemplary character and selfless service in the wake of the 9-11 event."

"What positive things came out of 9-11?" he asked.

I replied, "Many people have reassessed what is important in life. We have realized just how precious life is—that there are no guarantees of what tomorrow will bring—so we need to live life more fully today." The cameras continued to capture the launch celebration.

You may be asking yourself, "What would possess a 45-year-old, not-so-spring chicken, to get on a bicycle and ride across America? Was it a mid-life crisis, or was it something else?" I like to say that I was out of my mind—and into my heart.

It all began with the 9-11-01 terrorist attacks on the World Trade Center in New York and the Pentagon in Washington, D.C. As I watched the chaos unfold on television that day and the days that followed, I first experienced utter disbelief. I was in shock. I grieved for those who lost their lives and for those loved ones left behind. I also felt anxious and fearful about what would happen next. Then, in the next moments, I watched a paradox unfold. Selfish interests and desires yielded to selfless service. Firefighters, police and other emergency rescue workers sprang into action. I saw people risk their own lives in hopes of saving the lives of strangers. I was moved by the extraordinary courage and selfless service they showed. My fear dissipated, and my heart opened with love and compassion.

Other amazing events began to unfold in the weeks that followed. Ordinary people did extraordinary things. Young and old people across the nation and the world, put their own lives and ambitions on hold for a brief period of time to help in any way they could. People stood in lines for hours to give blood. People drove across the country with supplies that they had collected through the generosity of people in their own communities. Children drew pictures, wrote cards and raised money to send to the New York rescue workers and to the rescue workers from their own hometowns. People from around the world expressed their emotional support, prayer support and good wishes.

People shared their own unique talents, skills and abilities to help ease the pain of other human beings. For a moment in time, no one cared about the color of a person's skin or the name of his or her god. Christians, Muslims, and Jews put aside their holy war to pray together. People of all colors and creeds worked together side by side. People simply wanted to help.

A few days after the event, the Dalai Lama shared this wisdom: "Any violence will only increase the cycle of violence…Any problem with humanity should be solved in a humanitarian way, and nonviolence is the human way of approaching a target…. I think all religions have the same potential to strengthen human values and to develop general harmony."

Pope Paul II delivered a prayer on September 16, 2001, in Frosinone, Italy, to a crowd of 40,000 people: "…all the children of this great nation (America)…do not fall into the temptation of hatred and violence but rather to commit themselves to justice and peace."

Newspapers, television and radio stations covered human-interest stories about kind and generous acts of people giving of themselves. I received a barrage of emails of inspiring stories, prayers, poems and possibilities generated from around the planet. Suddenly the world seemed to be very small as people reached out to one another in this time of need.

President George W. Bush and New York Mayor Rudolph Giuliani became healers of a nation in need as they offered prayers and emotional support during a time of great madness and confusion. I had a feeling of connection with humanity unlike any that I had ever experienced in my lifetime.

Whatever your personal experience with the events of 9-11 and the ensuing war on terrorism, at the heart of it are universal truths that can help us through tragedies like these—truths that we can invoke in all areas of our lives to create the peace and happiness that we desire. These simple truths are revealed throughout this book.

Cycling for 70 days on country roads at an average speed of 13 miles per hour was a very rich experience for me. Because there is no way to fully appreciate the beauty of America behind the windshield of a car traveling at 75 miles per hour on interstate highways, I gained a whole new appreciation for the beauty and diversity of America and its peoples. Also, spending five to six hours a day in the saddle cycling across the country gave me precious time to be alone with my thoughts—time that I rarely allow myself in the everyday *busy-ness* of life. While I was riding, I gained extraordinary insight and clarity into what each of us can do to achieve peace of mind even in turbulent times. I received a glimpse of the types of insights that Einstein must have received as he ran his "thought experiments," or that Buddha received while he was sitting under the bodhi tree contemplating the nature of suffering, or that Gandhi and Dr. Martin Luther King, Jr., received while they were thinking deeply about our divine nature and right to equality; or that Jesus received in the wilderness. In times of prolonged silence and deep contemplation, pure and simple answers eventually come.

Ray of Hope: Inspiring Peace - Insights on Chaos and Consciousness While Bicycling Across America is the first book to present practical solutions for creating unshakeable peace of mind and peace in the world, by applying proven universal scientific and spiritual principles, in an easy-to-understand, conversational way. *Ray of Hope: Inspiring Peace* will:

- Define in simple terms a clear picture of what both science and spirituality have identified as timeless laws and principles that govern our lives and the universe as a whole.
- Demonstrate how and why the principles work.
- Provide thoughts to ponder and/or practical action steps to practice in order to experience the principles working in everyday life.

Pieces of a magnificent puzzle will be revealed mile by mile as I share about events along the route. At the end of your journey through the book, the pieces will be assembled into a beautiful mosaic that identifies and connects all the practical, essential principles learned for creating peace and happiness in your life.

I promise to stimulate your mind and warm your heart as you join me on this extraordinary journey. As a side benefit, if you have never experienced heartland America on a bicycle, now's your chance to enjoy a real treat.

Many blessings on your journey.

Chapter 1
Step into Your Fear and Do It

Ray, Lyn, Dominic and Joe at launch with friends July 4th, 2002.

On September 11, 2002, one year after the devastating terrorist attacks on New York City and Washington, D.C., I stood on Ellis Island gazing at the Statue of Liberty. It was a sunny and windy afternoon with scattered puffs of clouds gracing the sky. My heart felt wide open because of the emotional remembrance ceremonies I had attended earlier. I wondered to myself what our future would be like. New York is a different place today from the New York that I was born into 46 years ago. The statuesque World Trade Center towers that I watched rise from nothing during my youth no longer left their exclamation marks on the Manhattan skyline. It is mind boggling that these symbols of power and opulence vanished in an instant through a monstrous act of senseless destruction.

I wondered what the powers to be would choose to erect in their place. New Yorkers expressed mixed feelings. Some people want to build another bold symbol of strength and lavishness towering to heights surpassing any structure yet created in the world. One concept brought forth places the world's tallest spire as the central structure of a commercial office complex. When I saw this concept, I wondered to myself, "Why create another inviting target for terrorists—within or outside the U.S.—to salivate over?"

Another group wants to create a memorial to commemorate all those who lost their lives so senselessly. This would also serve as a place where people could go to continue their healing while learning ways to prevent hate and violence and to create peace. My hope is that a blending of the head and heart will prevail. On the constructive side, I consider how different the New Yorkers of today seem from those of a year ago. Those often aloof and callous seemed warmer and friendlier than I remembered as a child. I sense that the heart and soul of the Big Apple has transformed.

Standing there, I reminisced about my childhood growing up in New York State. Born in the Bronx, I was moved upstate to Schenectady when a baby. Taking the train into New York City several times a year to visit my relatives, my mom repeatedly reviewed the code of the city, "Don't talk to strangers and don't look a person in the eye." I remembered violating the code when I tried to look directly at people in the subway cars only to see each of them obeying the code and gazing blankly upward at the strategically placed advertising posters. Advertisers masterfully placed ads for their wares above head level in alignment with the New Yorkers' code of never looking a person in the eye.

Little did unsuspecting New Yorkers know that for this 2002 cycling trip to the Big Apple, my goal was to violate the code again at every opportunity—this time creating different results. Hindus say that the eyes are the windows to the soul. I decided that I was going to talk with as many people as I could, look them in the eyes, and peer into the beauty of their souls. I was amazed with the results. As I rode the subway this trip, most of the people that I looked at and struck up a conversation with were willing to both look me in the eyes and to share their thoughts.

I reflected on how far I had come in my life with all its twists and turns. I then reflected on the immigrants who had stood on Ellis Island where I was now standing, as they gazed at Lady Liberty and thought about the freedom that she symbolized to them—a freedom they personally craved. Like an immigrant who had embarked on a new life in a new world, I reviewed the seemingly insurmountable project that I had begun seven months ago to plan: Bicycle 3,369 miles from Phoenix in order to arrive at Ground Zero by September 11, 2002. All the challenges that Lyn and I faced and the aches, pains and physical discomfort that I experienced along the way were well worth being here today. Our Cycling 4 Peace journey was a celebration of the principles of freedom, equality and unity that have been so precious to Americans. And it seemed like only yesterday that our trip across America began.

It was 5:30 a.m., Friday, July 4, 2002. It was a typical Phoenix summer day—sunny, hot and dry with hardly a cloud in the bright blue sky. The weather forecast the night before predicted a decrease in the temperature from the sweltering 109 degrees that we had experienced at the beginning of the week. Despite the prevalent, "Oh, but it's a dry heat!" thinking, any way it's cut, anything in three digits is hot. This day, it was supposed to cool down to a mere 105 degrees. Lyn and I began the 35-mile drive from our home in Gilbert to our launch site in downtown Phoenix when the sun had been up less than half an hour. Now it was fast approaching 100 degrees. Even in the air-conditioned comfort of our 1991 Toyota 4-Runner, I was sweating. But maybe the sweat didn't have so much to do with the temperature as with that upon which we were about to embark.

We had been up until 2:00 a.m. trying feverishly to complete packing. Even with all our hard work, we still had more packing to do before we could finally leave Phoenix for our 80-day journey. Never before had we packed for such a long trip.

We were both stressing out about all the logistics and possibilities. Additionally, Lyn was stressed about all the loose ends still not tied down. The short amount of time that we had had to plan the trip meant that she was not able to finalize arrangements for all the places to stay or the towns in which we were going to speak. We hadn't even been able to set up our laptop properly to send and receive emails and make website updates while on the road. I was stressed about how, on only two hours' sleep, I was going to endure the physical demands of 35 miles biking on the first day from downtown Phoenix to Fountain Hills and then having to finish packing before we could finally leave town the following day. Additionally, I was worried about cycling from Fountain Hills to Payson, one of the toughest days of the whole journey. We were both stressed out about how my two boys, Dominic (13) and Joe (11), would do for the next 10 days squeezed into the back seat of a truck filled to the brim with luggage, supplies, and a cooler jammed between them.

At one point in our drive to downtown Phoenix, Lyn and I looked at each other in silence. During the five years that we had been together, we had become proficient at reading each other's thoughts. The unspoken verbiage ran like this: "Are you sure you really want to do this? Are we nuts? How are we going to live on the road for 80 days? What is going to happen to our business? What is going to happen to our relationship — will it strengthen or will it tear apart?" The tension could be cut with a knife.

We couldn't turn back now, having already announced our intentions to the world. Newspapers had written about our journey. Radio stations had featured us on talk shows. Television stations had given us prime time coverage in the midst of their priority coverage of the war on terrorism. We had emailed our plans to our distribution list of thousands of names. Friends had contributed money and items that we requested for our project. We had even committed to write a weekly column for our local paper. In my mind we were obligated to do it. Weren't we?

I must admit, however, that several conflicting thoughts had crossed my mind. "They would understand if we decided to turn around now. They already think we are out of our minds, closing the doors of our business for over 80 days. Maybe I could fake an illness or injury. As a child I was a master at getting sick if I was afraid to do something. I was convincing then, so why not now? The saddle sores that had developed during my training to get in shape a month ago could have been showstoppers anyway if they didn't heal in time. Come to think of it, that would have been a good way out. Boy, did I miss a great opportunity." This inner noise was all the product of my ego's voice screaming to protect itself from fear of the unknown. That other, more calm, inner voice that had presented the idea in the first place responded quietly, clearly and succinctly, "You need to do this!" Deep inner knowing silenced the fear and overrode Ego's voice.

After what seemed like an eternity, we arrived at the Civic Plaza in downtown Phoenix at 6:10 a.m. and parked the truck south of the complex. The building blocked my view of the plaza so I couldn't see if anyone had arrived for our sendoff. I thought to myself, "What if no one shows up? Maybe people don't care what we are doing and what we have to say." Then I decided that it didn't matter. "Whoever shows up is perfect." In spite of all this inner dialogue, Lyn and I moved into action as soon as the truck stopped.

I took the recumbent bicycle off the truck's rear rack. This eight-foot-long bike was awkward to handle. As I struggled to take it off, sweat flowed profusely down my face. Lyn handed me my bike helmet and gloves. Putting them on and strapping the bike bag and hydration water pack to the rear bike rack, I felt a little like an Apollo astronaut preparing to blast off for the first time into outer space.

Duane, a long-time friend of mine, had loaned me this recumbent bicycle only four weeks prior to our launch date, suggesting that alternating its use with my regular road bike might relieve some of the pain of being in the saddle on my regular road bike for five to six hours a day. It had worked well while I was healing from the saddle sores during training the previous month, allowing me to sit in a more relaxed position, as in a chair, legs in front and buttocks the only thing in contact with the seat. It provided great crotch relief at critical times. Recumbent cyclists affectionately call traditional bicycles "wedgies." If you have ever experienced the playful, yet painful, gift of a "wedgie" as a child you have an idea to what they are referring.

I had logged only 125 miles on the recumbent bike during training and still had not mastered its little quirks and idiosyncrasies. I chose to use it instead of my 22-year-old road bike that first day of the journey in order to take advantage of the flat 35-mile terrain between Phoenix and Fountain Hills and to get more comfortable with it before I got up to the higher elevations and rolling hills.

A television reporter took me aside for an interview as soon as we reached the top of the plaza steps. Next, he took Lyn aside to get her perspective. That gave me time to make the rounds, hugging old and new friends who had come to lend their support at this ungodly hour on a holiday morning. Actually, it felt quite godly as I connected with these great human beings one by one. Included were my minister, Joel, and his wife, Kyra, and other friends Mike and Jacquie, Ed and Roberta, Perci and Bryson, Steve, Firefighter Captain Chris Ketterer, Janet (the mother of my children) and her friend, Angie.

There were also others present who had heard us on radio, television, or at the Phoenix Fire Station Chat a few nights before. For example, 16-year-old Jeremy and his family were there. He was organizing a "Hands and Hearts" effort to unite Americans across the country in a tribute to those who had lost their lives as a result of the 9-11 events. Even as he drew inspiration from our project, I drew inspiration from his. We fed each other's energy. We hugged.

I also hugged Phil, who had lost his son, Terrence, in the Trade Center tragedy. I suppose Phil came out to give a little more closure to wounds still open and healing with regard to his son. We shared tears as we embraced in a moment of mutual support and compassion. It seems to me that people hug each other more since 9-11. In any case, it was certainly the 9-11 crisis that had brought this group together this day to move our relationships to new levels.

This project was bigger than just Lyn and me. People were eager to help. They thirsted for anything that gave them even a glimmer of hope—of positive news and possibility in the midst of the media coverage of the ensuing war on terrorism. Truth is: Anyone could have done this ride. It is just that we chose to trust and follow our hearts to DO something positive and different in response to what was happening in the world. Many have followed their inner guidance to take other remarkable actions. Many more have received inner guidance but have chosen to let fear and doubt stop them. I made a decision to step *into* my fear and just do it. I have learned that every time I step into a fear, I elevate my mind to a new level of possibility. When I successfully overcome one fear, future fear-provoking situations have fewer negative effects on me.

Anyone could have done this ride.
It is just that we chose to trust and follow our hearts
to DO something positive and different
in response to what was happening in the world...
. . . every time I step into a fear,
I elevate my mind to a new level of possibility.

With our 6:30 a.m. launch time fast approaching, I shared a few words of thanks with our friends, old and new. I also read them the *It's Time!* poem that I wrote a few days after the 9-11 event, one which we would also share with people on our cross-country journey. I felt deeply connected to each person there. Our hearts opened up with love, compassion and support. And now 6:30 a.m. launch time had arrived! Although I wanted to savor the moment of embrace in the familiar and comforting arms of friends, it was time to venture into the unknown.

My heart pounded faster because of the adrenaline rush caused by that fear of the unknown. Also, I secretly worried about crashing the recumbent bike. I still lacked confidence in my abilities to control the unwieldy eight-foot monster. It was awkward for me to get moving from a standing start. Talk about stepping into my fear! I could hear the television news reporter leading his story with, "Cycling klutz crashes for peace! Report at six."

Thoughts of uncertainty and self-doubt rushed my mind. "Could I really ride 3,000 miles on a bike?" The most I had ever ridden was 500 miles, and that was over 25 years ago. "What if I fail? How will I face these dear friends if I fail? I would let them down. How would I face myself in the mirror? I would let myself down." I was amazed at the tremendous amount of self-inflicted pressure to fulfill both my expectations and the expectations of others.

Having discussed my vision of this trip with many people before beginning, I am sure that some with whom I shared feared tragic possibilities looming around various corners. For instance, I recalled my dear Aunt Sadie's response from Long Island when I called to tell her about this exciting idea. A little less than enthusiastic about the prospects of my trip, she responded, "Raymond, don't do it!" So much for unconditional love and support! Do you suppose this had something to do with the time, as a senior in high school, I surprised her by riding my bike 250 miles from my home in Schenectady, New York, to her home in Elmont, Long Island, showing up on her doorstep unannounced? The look on her face then was shock and total disbelief. It took her more than a few minutes for it to settle in that "little Raymond" had ridden his bike across New York State to get there!

My relatives weren't the only source of doubts. During the months leading up to the launch, my engineering mind contemplated the many things that could go wrong on a journey such as this: mechanical failure, physical body problems of all types, severe weather, and accidents. I asked myself a question that I learned from Dale Carnegie's book *How to Stop Worrying and Start Living*, "What is the worst that could happen?"

The answer didn't give me much reassurance as my ego responded with, "That's easy—being roadkill somewhere deep in the Appalachians of Kentucky." Thanks a lot!

As the moment of truth arrived, my legs began to tremble. I realized that I had done all that I could to prepare. As with all things, there is a point where one has planned all one can plan and it is time to take the first action step. I had weight trained for seven months in the gym and had ridden my bikes 1,500 miles during the previous three months. I was as ready as I could be. The moment of truth had come. It was time!

Television camera rolling, I eased the recumbent down the steps of the Civic Plaza to the street below. Mounting the bike, I lined up behind Captain Chris Ketterer of the Phoenix Fire Department, our escort, in his shiny red hook-and-ladder fire truck. Dominic and Joe got their bikes from their mother's truck and joined me for the ceremonial first few miles of Day One. Peter, a newfound friend, accompanied me on the first 35-mile leg from Phoenix to Fountain Hills. Others had told me that they would try to come and ride a few miles with me, but Peter was the only one who actually showed up on his bike. Something was clear to me now. This Cycling 4 Peace project was to be primarily the journey of one man and his supportive family to connect souls across the nation.

I straddled the bike, sat down, stretched my trembling right leg out, slid my foot into the toe clip, took a deep breath, and pushed off. To my surprise I had forgotten to tighten the seat. It slid back nearly beyond my reach of the pedals. Could it be that my worst nightmare was about to happen already? The bike swayed radically from side to side as I worked to compensate while clipping in my other foot. The seat shifted forward and backward with each stroke. I had wanted to look my best for the crowd and the camera, but so much for cool! Wow, what a way to begin! I remember thinking, "I hope this isn't a bad omen of the shape of things to come."

Once out of view of the crowd, I got off the bike to adjust and tighten the seat. Continuing east on Washington Street, I spotted a cycling club of over 40 riders coming toward us. A few days prior to the launch I had received an email from their club president stating that they would try to make it to our launch as part of their day's ride. He had lived his word. We waved to each other in a gesture of support and acknowledgment as we passed, then continued on our separate journeys.

My legs stopped trembling after a few miles and I found myself getting into a rhythm and being more present to the task at hand. We took it easy the first five miles so that my boys could enjoy a casual pace. Five miles was their limit. Their mom, following in her vehicle as planned, waited for them to reach their limit, then stopped and loaded their bikes back into her truck.

Captain Ketterer then asked the kids a tough question, "Do you want to ride in the fire truck?" Tough, right! In a flash they climbed into his hook and ladder. At that point Peter and I picked up the pace to the Phoenix city limit, as that was the end of the line for our fire-truck escort. I hugged the big brute and thanked him for all his support. It was he who wrote us the testimonial letter which helped open the doors to fire stations across the country so that we could hold public presentations focused on "Creating Peace of Mind in Turbulent Times." He also furnished us with videotape footage that captured the experiences of the Phoenix Fire Department's Emergency Search and Rescue Team at Ground Zero, NYC. These we would distribute to fire stations across America. Captain Ketterer even loaned us a flashing light bar for the back of our truck so that we could be more visible and safer in traffic. Thanks to him, I avoided being melded with the pavement or adhering to a bumper somewhere en route. This trip would only prove successful due to people like Chris. So many people were generous with their time, talents and treasure. And they will not be soon forgotten!

By the end of our 70-day journey, I realized that all those initial fears were for naught. I should have known better than to have put so much energy into worrying. Over 90 percent of the things that we fear never materialize. The Cycling 4 Peace trip reminded me of this and other important life principles. It does not make sense to waste time wallowing in the past, worrying about the future, or fearing our every step. What a waste of precious time and mental energy. Through reading this chronicle and learning from my life lessons, I hope that you, too, can make your life journey more peaceful and joyous!

Over 90 percent of the things that we fear never materialize.

The first step of anything which you are being inspired to do is to . . .

Step into Your Fear and Do It

Thoughts to Ponder:
Chapter 1 - Step into Your Fear and Do It

1. Identify a goal or idea that you feel that you are to express.

2. How would you feel if you didn't do it? How would you feel if you did?

3. What fear is holding you back?

4. What is the worst that could happen if you stepped into your fear to do it? What is the best that could happen?

5. How could you improve on the worst if it happened?

6. Which one step into your fear are you willing to take? When will you do it?

You can purchase and enjoy the rest of *Ray of Hope: Inspiring Peace* in both print book and eBook formats. To order go to:

https://www.createspace.com/3953170

Bibliography and Suggested Reading

Blanchard, Ken and Spencer Johnson, *The One Minute Manager*, Berkley, 1982.

Blanchard, Ken and Spencer Johnson, *The New One Minute Manager*, William Morrow, 2015.

Byrne, Rhonda. *The Secret*, Beyond Words, 2006.

Canfield, Jack, with Janet Switzer. *The Success Principles: How to Get from Where You Are to Where You Want to Be*, Collins, 2005.

Carnegie, Dale. *How to Stop Worrying and Start Living*, Simon and Schuster, 1984.

Carnegie, Dale. *How to Win Friends and Influence People*, Dale Carnegie Associates, 1964.

Collins, James and Jerry Porras. *Built to Last: Successful Habits of Visionary Companies*, Harper Business, 1994.

Collins, Jim. *Good to Great: Why Some Companies Make the Leap...and Others Don't*, Harper Business, 2001.

Covey, Stephen. *The 7 Habits of Highly Effective People,* Fireside, 1989.

Dyer, Wayne. *The Power of Intention*, Hay House, 2005.

Emoto, Masaru. *The Hidden Messages in Water*, Beyond Words, 2004.

Franklin, Benjamin. *Benjamin Franklin: The Autobiography and Other Writings*, Penguin Books, 1986.

Gerber, Michael. *The E-Myth Revisited: Why Most Small Businesses Don't Work and What to Do About It,* Harper Business, 1995.

Goodstein, Leonard, Timothy Nolan, and J. William Pfeiffer. *Applied Strategic Planning: A Comprehensive Guide*, McGraw-Hill, 1993.

Greenleaf, Robert. *Servant Leadership: A Journey Into the Nature of Legitimate Power and Greatness*, Paulist Press, 1977.

Heider, John. *The Tao of Leadership: Leadership Strategies for a New Age*, Bantam Books, 1985.

Hersey, Paul. *The Essentials of Situational Leadership*, Leadership Studies, Inc., 1986.

Hicks, Esther, and Jerry Hicks. *The Law of Attraction: The Basics of the Teachings of Abraham*, Hay House, 2006.

Hill, Napoleon. *The Law of Success*, Napoleon Hill Foundation, 53rd printing, 1997.

Hill, Napoleon. *Think and Grow Rich*, Faucett, 1937.

Madaghiele, Ray. *Ray of Hope: Inspiring Peace – Insights On Chaos and Consciousness While Bicycling Across America*, TLC and Create Space, 2012.

Reck, Ross, Brian Long. *The Win-Win Negotiator: How to Negotiate Favorable Agreements that Last*, Pocket Books, 1987.

Tolle, Eckhart. *The Power of Now*, Namaste Publishing, 2004.

INDEX

Energize Your Business

Made in the USA
Monee, IL
18 June 2023

35807892R00148